-DRUMMERS-

Rites of Passage on the Parade Route

Book I—The Trainee
Chronicles of a Teenage
Syncopated Drummer

BRIAN MCBRIDE

PublishAmerica
Baltimore

First printing

PublishAmerica has allowed this work to remain exactly as the author intended, verbatim, without editorial input.

ISBN: 1-60672-451-7 (softcover)
ISBN: 978-1-4489-1503-3 (hardcover)
PUBLISHED BY PUBLISHAMERICA, LLLP
www.publishamerica.com
Baltimore

Printed in the United States of America

For Marvin Marker,
The Pied-Piper of Long Beach

Acknowledgments

I am indebted to the following people for their contributions to this book:

To my mother Karen McBride, friend Connie Nanasy (Robert Sainburg's mother) and Mark McMullen (fellow drummer) for their wonderful assistance in the editing of this book.

To Robert Sainburg for bringing me to LBJCB and for being my friend for over 40 years.

To my wife Janis for her invaluable input and loving support from the very beginning.

FOREWORD

At first glance this book may appear to be the writings of an aspiring author reliving the glory days of his youth. Some may think the author is trying to find a niche market on his way to fame and fortune. I submit that it's neither. I count the author, Brian McBride as one of my closest long term personal friends. What he has written about here goes beyond teenage high jinks. It is a story of finding oneself, a chance at redemption and hitting the big time as a youth.

The mid 1970's found America in turmoil with gas shortages, the ending of the Vietnam War and the continuation of the cold war with the Soviets. The American political system was being challenged as was the moral fabric of the nation.

As teenagers, all of the world's big problems were beyond our immediate reality. Life in the suburbs, however, was large and complicated. High school life then was as full of drama as it is today. My personal life was in turmoil as an alcoholic father left his family behind in ruins. The years of emotional neglect behind the "closed doors" of the American dream in suburbia had started to take a devastating toll. Being a latch key kid was a hard reality.

As a 15 year old I found myself without direction, parental guidance and no real friends. I was a nobody in a world of somebodies.

But the drum section and band that you will read about in the pages ahead literally saved my life. It was the drum section that took me in, encouraged me, showed me what pride, discipline, teamwork and hard work was all about. These basic principles were the very foundation of the traits that have carried me through to where I am today.

These pages are not just about teenage high jinks and youths gone wild. They are stories of coming of age, of first kisses, first cars, first beers and finally being socially accepted. It is about the adventures and the maturing of teenagers into young men.

The author, my good friend Brian has masterfully captured the essence of those days of the mid to late 1970's. He remains true to the times and has done a superb job of writing what life was like in suburban Southern California for disenfranchised kids. Kids who just didn't fit in at high school as a jock, surfer or a stoner. Many teenagers of that day found themselves in a gray zone no-mans land. This book is the tale of a small select group that got out of no-mans land and then became drummers in the Long Beach Junior Concert Band and later in the Last Generation of Syncopated Drummers. These pages will bring back fond memories of those days for all of us that grew up back in the 1970's and were a part of the marching band scene. For those that came after, the book serves as a "historical record" for a special time in our lives. The author provides a gift for you to share a little of what those times were like.

Many of the names you will read about still remain close personal friends. The fallout from those days would last to present times as the brotherhood of syncopated drummers still remains strong 30 plus years later. This book is only the beginning of a lifetime saga of laughs, good times and the sharing of life's experiences among a tight knit group of boys who became drummers and later successful adults.

Mark McMullen
LBJCB, LGSD Snare drummer, Class of 1976

Oh, the brave music of a distant drum!

—Omar Khayyam, Poet

PROLOGUE

Huntington Beach Parade, July 4, 1977

You glance over the shoulder of the snare drummer marching in front of you and, trying desperately to catch your breath, look ahead at the parade route and into the abyss. The congested street spans for miles into the distance and to the syncopated drummers playing cadences in the ninety-degree summer heat, this is nothing short of death...it is a hellish battlefield. The drummers have been pounding out cadences for at least a mile without a break and have pushed their bodies to the limits. You figure there is still half a parade to go, plus the drummer circle-up and you don't know how you are going to make it. The heat rolls in waves across the street like a black phantom and you fight desperately just to hold it all together, your mind numbed with exhaustion. *I'm so thirsty,* you think, pushing the image of a cool glass of water right out of your head. Every time you get to the brink during a parade like this, you wonder why you keep coming back to it like some kind of obsession. *Why didn't I just go surfing in the crystal blue ocean,* you think as you gaze out from under your shako visor down the endless parade route, *instead, here I am marching across burning asphalt in a band uniform playing tenor drum with Jeff, Greg, Karl, Joe and twenty other drummers!* You adjust your gloves and tenor mallets, preparing for another brutal round of playing drum cadences. *You just had to prove it to yourself,* your mind answers as you take in deep breathes through your nose, *you just had to show these guys that you have what it takes to be a syncopated drummer!*

Streams of sweat trickle down your back and legs and your polished white band shoes feel like hot irons against your feet as you stand at parade rest in a marching 'traffic jam,' waiting for the Long Beach Junior Concert Band to start moving forward. Your band uniform feels like a damp, scratchy burlap bag covering your entire body, the stiff collar pressing against your throat, the heavy cloth weighing down your arms with every upward swing of your mallets. The shako on your head is a plastic ring of torture, trapping the July heat onto your scalp, and your drum...it suddenly feels so heavy on your shoulder. The glare of the sun reflects brightly off the chrome bumper of a car, almost blinding you as you try to make out the chaotic mess of distorted images up ahead...horses, parade floats, flag drill teams and clowns...vintage convertible Cadillac's and squads of old men in Shriner caps, all converging in one congested blur as the mass of screaming spectators with patriotic streamers and balloons close in on both sides like a vise-grip. *No escape,* you think with the dread of knowing the physical toll you will suffer in the second half of the parade. The diesel smoke and stink of horse manure makes you want to vomit. The shrill blast of those damned plastic horns pierce your head like a spike. You start calculating your chances of making it to the end and wonder how much longer you can hammer down on your tenor drum in this heat...how long before the legs buckle?

"Forward, MARCH!" barks the drum major and two hundred band members drone forward like a massive teen-army, marching to the click of the rim beat. *Only one way out,* you think as the drunken July fourth crowd yells, "Come on drummers...more, MORE!!" *got to march straight through, get to the buses and the circle-up...please Lord, just let me make it to the end.* The head drummer Lonny throws out the hand signal, yelling, "Two through five!" and with four clicks of his drum sticks every snare, tenor, bass, and cymbal player raises their arms high overhead and digs in with every ounce of strength they have.

It is a brutal, crazy parade on this day and two drummers collapse from the heat at the circle-up, but you have survived. "Well done boys," Lonny would tell us later back on the bus...but there were no *boys* to be found standing at the end of that parade.

"Oh when I look back now,
That summer seemed to last forever.
And if I had the choice,
Ya—I'd always wanna be there.
Those were the best days of my life."
—Bryan Adams, Musician

CHAPTER 1

Rob and I stood behind a meticulously-trimmed juniper hedge along the gravel driveway of Sunnyside Mortuary, trying to figure out our next move. "So," Rob turned to me and whispered, "you got the dare once we're inside?" Holding a hand across my forehead to block the bright sun piercing through the clouds, I scanned the mortuary grounds looking for an entry into the building and any sign of life... *Ha! Funny one Bri,* I thought, *signs of life in a mortuary, that's good.* Spotting an opened door with no security guard or hearse driver in sight, I ducked down behind the waist-high bushes onto my knees, and turned towards Rob.

"Yeah," I whispered back, "we get inside, find a dead person in the darkest most scary corner of the whole mortuary, and I stand next to it...er, him or her, for five minutes." I motioned to Rob with a raised hand, pointing towards the doorway to make sure he saw the way in. I then shifted my body weight and placed my fingers on the ground like an Olympic athlete, preparing to make a run for the open door. Rob did the same as I continued to answer his question. "If I do it and then calmly walk back into the light without freaking out, you'll stop bugging me about seeing your so-called 'bad-ass drummers' for as long as we..."

Rob interrupted, "But, if you lose and go running off screaming like a little girl, then you have to come with me to band practice tomorrow night." I shook my head and stared back at Rob, who was grinning with that familiar 'gotcha' look that I had seen a thousand times before. I wondered why I had agreed to this silly dare in the first place. Rob was fifteen and I was sixteen and we were getting too old for this kind of stuff.

"Yeah, yeah," I reluctantly replied, "I'll go to band practice with you...but I'm NOT going to lose!" As if to change the subject, I pointed towards the black wrought-iron gate that we would have to pass through to get to the mortuary door. Rob affirmed with a nod. A bird whipped by overhead and a motorcycle blasted down Cherry Street behind us which made us jump. "All clear," I whispered, "but you go first since this was your idea." Rob scoffed in response. He then stood and shrugged his shoulders taking two steps towards the edge of the bush. He whispered, "Banzai," and stepped out into the open on his tip-toes, sneaking up to the stone wall that surrounded the premises. Attempting to keep his shoes from crunching across the gravel driveway, he moved slowly as if walking under water and it reminded me of that cartoon episode where Bugs Bunny sniffs ether. Sometimes I couldn't tell when Rob was joking or just being himself because he was the biggest natural goofball without even trying. This time his cartoon grin gave him away and I chuckled as he swung his arms out slowly, lifting each leg in exaggerated steps. I cupped my hands around my mouth, whispering, "Come back you waaa-bit," and he started busting up.

Rob made his way to the edge of the stone wall and up to the open iron gate. I noticed that the top of his head nearly reached the 'Hearse Entrance Only' sign overhead. I guess you could say that we were opposites physically. Rob was long-limbed more than muscular, with cumbersome yet aggressive movements. He had a frizzy 'Brillo' patch of short-cropped sandy brown hair and a mouth full of braces. His fierce blue eyes were set in a sloping brow that gave his every expression a look of anguish beyond his years. His tan Levi's cord pants were clean and pressed, his white T-shirt neatly tucked in behind his brass belt buckle. He definitely looked more put-together than my shaggy appearance. By contrast, I was the shorter but more agile one, always trying to strut around doing tricks on my skateboard like some kind of cool surfer dude. My barely combed sun-bleached blond hair had grown down to the collar of my striped Hang-Ten shirt and my jeans had holes in the knees from too many falls on my skateboard. *Just a freckle-faced chump with peach-fuzz coming in over your lip,* I thought, as I recalled Rob's Mom always calling me 'Opie' because I somehow reminded her of Ron Howard from the Andy Griffith Show. *Oops, Opie grew his hair.* I thought with a devilish delight.

Sliding up against the stone wall Rob stood still, raising his hand slowly in the universal 'standby' gesture and I could see his eyes tracking the area in front of him to make sure the coast was clear. Same stealth tactics we'd seen a thousand times on TV cop shows and loved to imitate. His eyes darted back in my direction. Spotting my position about twenty yards back behind the shrubs, he motioned me forward. I couldn't figure out why we were acting like a SWAT team on this when all we had to deal with were dead people and maybe a couple of groundskeepers. The place looked deserted so far and I wasn't worried because I knew we could bullshit our way out of there even if we did run into someone. We could just say that we were visiting a deceased relative or something.

I rushed across the gravel to join up behind him at the wide opening of the gate. Rob turned to me and whispered, "You go check the side door. Make sure we can get in that way." We didn't want to go in through the front lobby. Our goal was to sneak in and find the room where the corpses were kept. The reality of that possibility was just now hitting us.

"No way dude, you go." I said.

"No shit, no way! We're probably gonna see a fricking dead person, man!" Rob said nervously, "This is the real deal!" A look of mental calculation swept across his face. "What's the worst that can happen?" he said, as if he were trying to convince himself more than me. "So we see a dead person, so what? We'll get over the first shock and it'll be no big deal." Rob then seemed to realize that it was ME, not him, that would have to actually stand next to a dead person. "Besides," he continued, as if totally relieved, "YOU'RE the one that has to take the dare. This is our big chance, man, come on let's go!"

"Okay-okay," I replied impatiently, "but let's at least both go inside at the same time. That's only fair." Rob gave me a mischievous grin and then pushed me in front of him. "No, you go!" he whispered.

"No, YOU go," I snapped, pushing him back. After a few seconds of sliding around in the gravel in a push fight, we continued forward with Rob in the lead. Moving past a row of polished black hearses we came up to the side entrance, pushed the door open, and stepped inside of the mortuary.

*   *   *

It was the last Saturday in January of 1976, and although it had rained all week, the rain had stopped and the sun was trying to burn through the huge clouds passing overhead. We had been sitting in Rob's Mom's living room, and although I was fine with just listening to the radio, Rob was bored stiff and trying to think of something exciting to do. That just about describes me and Rob to a tee... I was always the cautious one and Rob was always playing 'Mr. Adventure.' It was the break in the weather that must have motivated Rob to talk me into getting outside and that's when we agreed to walk over to the mortuary. I think we were short on ideas for new activities too, because Lord knows we had explored just about every corner of Lakewood since we were kids. Then Rob started talking about his drummers again, and came up with the idea of actually sneaking into the mortuary and his dead body dare. Even though I was reluctant as usual, I had to admit that checking out the inside of a place for dead people actually seemed like a cool idea. So, we got our butts off the living room couch and headed for the mortuary. We made the one-mile hike down the sidewalk, through the neighborhood, across the park and over an open grass field towards the mortuary.

I'd known Robert Peter Sainburg since 1965, back when we were both just little kids. This was longer than any other friend I had, so I guess you could say that Rob was my first real friend. We grew up in an upper middle class neighborhood in Lakewood California, which is a large suburb about twenty miles south of Los Angeles and ten miles inland from the sunny coast. As you enter Lakewood, the street signs display a futuristic greeting, 'Tomorrow's City Today,' but all we saw growing up there in the sixties and seventies were the last remnants of someone else's yesterday. It was as if the city were suspended between different eras in time. The old train tracks, drive-in theatres, go-cart raceways and corner markets were still there, but were slowly disappearing as the modern look of strip centers, malls and multiplex movie theatres emerged.

For a while though, my neighborhood seemed like one of the last places where the guy at the gas station actually pumped gas and checked under the hood for my Mom. We even still had the Helms Bakery truck bringing those great warm bread smells, the jingle-jingle of the ice-cream truck in the summer as you'd chase it down the street, and the milkman picking up your glass empties and delivering fresh dairy products right up to your front porch. I watched them making their rounds every day, but little did I know that these were the final deliveries in an era soon to be replaced by supermarkets, Seven-Eleven stores and self-serve gas stations. I was lucky to get a last glimpse of it though, before 'Mayberry' was torn down and the 'Brady Bunch' moved in.

Even though Rob and I lived in a decent neighborhood because our Dad's were doctors, we had problems like any other kids. Rob's parents split up when he was twelve, and because he had a mild speech impediment he was a target at school, enduring countless standoffs with the playground bullies. There were fistfights on a regular basis, but as Rob grew taller and stronger guys started backing off. He soon had a reputation for being a real hot-head at school. I on the other hand had no reputation at all. I hadn't adjusted too well in Catholic grammar school, with nuns yelling every day and slapping us kids with rulers if we were even the slightest bit restless after recess. They were always trying to push us down with their strict rules. It was supposed to be an 'excellent academic program,' but all I got from the experience was a bunch of low grades and a total lack of self-confidence. By the time

I got to high school I was all bottled up...way too shy to speak up in class or even talk to girls. Although we were opposites in many ways, Rob and I shared the common thread of feeling like misfits. We bonded at a young age, and even though we never talked about it, it was understood that we would always watch each others backs.

*   *   *

Once inside the darkened building the first thing I noticed was how quiet and still it was. "Creepy," whispered Rob and I nodded in agreement. There was no one around, and it seemed we could have walked off with just about anything we could carry, like a chair or an ashtray. I didn't really want to touch anything though and I couldn't figure out why the room we were standing in smelled like wet, rotten flowers. In fact, it looked exactly like a small flower shop.

"Look at this," Rob said, pointing to what looked like a rectangular elevator. We looked at each other, and our eyes widened as we realized what we were looking at.

"Holy crap!" I said, "it's for the caskets. They come from somewhere down below!" My hands were sweaty all of a sudden and I began wiping them on my jeans. "There must be a basement where the bodies are kept," I continued. "they embalm them down below, put 'em in the casket, and then lift them up here for the hearse!" I walked up to get a closer look. "Far out," was all that came out of my mouth. We'd never seen anything like it. We were positive that it was some kind of casket dumb-waiter.

"We'll have to try to get down there somehow," Rob said, and I shivered as if someone had just tickled my neck with a feather. Just then we heard voices outside and crunching gravel footsteps coming our way. I looked through a small window and saw two men dressed in black coats coming towards us. "Holy Moly, let's get out of here," I whispered, tapping Rob's shoulder impatiently. We slid through another doorway and walked down a long hallway going deeper into the mortuary, then stepped into what looked like a church. The ceiling was fifty feet high and there were religious statues all along the walls with huge stained glass windows overhead. We quietly stepped past a pipe-organ and up the center aisle when I noticed a corridor at the back of the altar leading somewhere beyond the church. "Over here," I whispered to Rob and we made our way to the corridor. We stopped at the entrance and I gasped as I looked at the cold grey marble walls on either side. The marble was cut in a perfect matrix of squares outlining each gravestone, and they were stacked six high and extended out into darkness. A sign on the wall read 'Mausoleum' and even though I didn't know what the word meant, it sent a chill up my spine.

"Man, this is wicked," I said under my breath.

Rob put his finger to his lips, "Ssshhhh," he hissed as he walked straight up the middle of the corridor, the bottoms of his feet reflecting off the white marble floor.

Yep, guess we're going all the way, I thought nervously, remembering the deep voice of the narrator in the

Haunted Mansion at Disneyland...elevator drops you down, and the voice says, "No windows, and no doors."

Walking a couple of paces behind Rob, I glanced in amazement at the shiny brass nameplates of the crypts. I tried to imagine the dried skin and bones lying still just behind the marble, dressed in faded clothing and dusty jewelry. The best I could comprehend of death was the thought of being trapped inside of a box against your will, unable to see, move, or breathe...never again to walk freely outside on a sunny day, feeling the warmth and the breeze against your skin, or breathing in the fresh air. I took a deep breath and felt glad to be alive...thankful that it wasn't me inside that box.

Some of the crypts had vases attached to them with fresh cut flowers. Rob pointed to one that was near the floor, the area below covered with cards and toys. It was that of a child who had died at age five. That one got to me the most, to think of a kid getting gypped like that, not getting to see his sixth birthday.

I noticed more hallways branching off on both sides of the main corridor, housing more crypts. It was like one big maze. *A maze of death,* I thought, as we walked to the end of the corridor. We stopped at the end and turned around, realizing that there were no doors, no elevator to take us down below, nothing...it was just a dead end. I wanted to get the hell out of there.

"Still no dead bodies in sight," Rob said. His words gave me a chill. Then I noticed that one of the hallways had yellow tape blocking it, indicating that the area was still under construction. I motioned to Rob and we walked up to the taped-off space.

"Whoa, these over here are all still empty!" I said, and pointed towards rows of hollow cells with no fancy marble covers...just dark concrete cubes waiting to be occupied. The window at the end was just a circular opening with no stained glass installed yet. It had a thin sheet of torn plastic tarp covering it with blue tape. The opening let in some light from outside, and a breeze had blown leaves onto the unfinished concrete floor. I started planning our escape, figuring out how we could get up to the window and crawl out of this place.

Rob pushed on my shoulder, pointing to one of the concrete honeycomb openings. "Come on Bri, climb inside one of them," he said, and I could tell by his expression that he was being serious. "Since we can't find a dead body, let's change the dare." He came in close to me and put his arm around my shoulder, like he was about to make me an offer that I couldn't refuse. "Since this spot right here is pretty dark and scary, the new dare is that you climb inside one of those holes and stay in there for five minutes. If you can lay still in there for that long, I promise not to ever mention band practice or the drummers for as long as we both shall live. What do ya say?"

I jerked away from Rob. "No way in hell! I'm not going in there!" *Screw it,* I thought, *I'll go to his stupid band practice, just get me the hell out of this place.* Rob grabbed my shirt and we started push fighting again, when a sudden noise made us stop. We stood frozen in place, barely able to breath. Something stirred from deep inside one of the empty concrete holes.

I had barely muttered "What the…" when in the same instant a solid wall of zigzagging feathers came at us…it was the most panicked flock of something straight out of hell that I'd ever seen!

"HO-LEE SHIIIT!!"

We both screamed bloody murder, and stumbled over each other like Keystone cops trying to get a running start. Finally my feet answered my brain and I started running as fast as I could, my Adidas flapping on the hard marble. Rob was right behind me breathing hard and saying, "shit-shit" over and over, as at least a hundred startled pigeons flew up. Some flew up to the ceiling and some escaped through the open window where they had come in. I don't know who was more terrified, the pigeons or us, but I'd never been so freaked out in my entire life!

We back-tracked up the corridor, running like track stars past the crypts and through the church. We tore out down the hallway towards the flower shop, bolting straight for the daylight of the door that we had first entered. We got to the doorway and my heart was pounding up in my throat. I stopped just short of the door, spotting two men in black coats standing right outside. "Dammit!" I whispered excitedly and put my hand up so that Rob would stop. Instead he rammed into me, causing my body to slam against the wall and sending a jolt of pain through my left elbow. "What?" he asked, and I pointed outside and replied, "Ssshhh!" as I rubbed my throbbing funny bone.

We were breathing hard and leaning against the wall just out of sight as I tried to figure out what the hell to do next. Maybe I was too freaked out to care, but something inside of me snapped and I turned to Rob and yelled, "Screw them, let's get the frick out of here!" We tore out the door and flew right past them, kicking up gravel behind us.

I think one of them shouted, "Hey!" but it didn't matter, our adrenaline was pumped so high that we could have jumped over a twenty-foot brick wall if we had to. They never would have caught us. We ran straight across the gravel driveway, back through the iron gate and over the large field of grass to the sidewalk along Cherry Avenue. We were halfway to Rob's house before we stopped to catch our breaths, and then we started laughing so hard that we were coughing and choking just to take in some air.

"You were so scared shitless, dude!" Rob finally said, catching his breath.

"Yeah right, who was the little wussie who ran first, huh?" We tried another push fight but were too tired to even lift an arm.

"I'm never going in that fricking place again," Rob said.

"No kidding!" I agreed, "Not until we have to, heh?"

We walked along Cherry Avenue up to Del Amo Boulevard, turning right towards Rob's house as we rehashed all that we had experienced in the mortuary. Dark clouds rolled overhead, and it looked like it might start raining. "Well man," I said, finally breathing normally, "how do you top that?"

"I don't know," Rob replied, "let's go eat something. My Mom's got some chicken in the fridge. Then we can take turns playing my drum set or something."

"Cool with me," I said. We were about two blocks from Rob's house and food sounded like a good idea.

"Speaking of drums," Rob said, and I knew what was coming next, "even though the dare got messed up, admit it…you did freak out in there." I glared at Rob, not needing to point out the obvious. "I know, I know," he continued, "even though I freaked too, the bet was that YOU would keep your cool no matter what." I didn't exactly follow Rob's logic at this point, but I was just so glad to be out of that mortuary that I caved and went along with it. "So," Rob continued, "I think that means that you have to come with me tomorrow night to band practice, right?"

I looked at Rob and thought about how he had kept pushing me on this question over the past couple of months, and how much I had resisted. He talked my ear off about this city marching band he had joined called the Long Beach Junior Concert Band. 'LBJCB' as he called it for short and it just sounded lame to me. Rob said he had found out about LBJCB from his Mom, Connie, who played piano in the Long Beach City College jazz band. She was at rehearsal one night and could hear LBJCB practicing in the distance at Long Beach Veteran's Stadium. She took Rob over there to check it out and that's when he got hooked. Rob had talked me into a lot of things through the years and although I had to admit that we usually had fun, sometimes it just didn't work out. I never forgot those karate lessons he talked me into in which I totally got my ass kicked by a dude twice my size, or sleeping on the dirt in the leaky tee-pees at Camp Oaks in the pouring rain, or the day Rob convinced me to go ice skating with him and I split my lip on the ice trying to race him. I felt that this time my resistance was justified, and I sure as hell wasn't going to let Rob trick me into seeing his lame-ass marching band! This is why the words felt so weird coming from my mouth when I finally said, "Alright, alright sure Rob, I'll go to the damn band practice with you."

"Bitchin!" Rob said excitedly and I couldn't believe how psyched-up he looked after I told him that I would go. "I'll ask Tom if he can give us a ride over to practice. He has a car and both of our houses are right on the way, so it shouldn't be a hassle." This time I didn't give Rob the excuse that I had used before, that I was already in Lakewood High School marching band and didn't get how a city youth band could be any better than the high school band. Rob swore every time though, that if I saw these syncopated drummers just once I'd be blown away. "Trust me dude, you're gonna wet your pants when you see this drum section. You've never seen anything like it!"

According to Rob, this drum section was known all over town as the 'thunder drummers,' because they were so loud you could hear them coming from miles away. Rob played the snare drum and I noticed that his hands were always beat up with blisters from playing in this drum section. I didn't understand what the big deal was and why he seemed so proud of his messed-up hands. He also wore a brown sweatshirt with the sleeves cut off at the elbows and gold lettering on the back that read 'Drummer—LBJCB.' He wore the sweatshirt every single day to school, and if anybody hassled him about it, they were in for a fight. Rob would tear your head off. Rob was totally dedicated to the drum section and it had actually gotten in the way of our friendship. Rob and I hadn't been hanging out nearly as much as we used to because he was always at band practice or on some weekend bus trip across the State performing with the band.

As we walked up to his house Rob stopped, turned to me and said, "Bri, come with me to just this one band practice. If you don't like what you see, there's no obligation whatsoever... I'll shut up, eat my shorts, and never bring it up to you again."

I hesitated, stalling my answer all the way up to Rob's front door, and as he opened it, I finally said with a grin, "I'll go, but you better get ready with the salt and pepper, because you're going to be eating those skivvies!"

CHAPTER 2

I stood on the front lawn of my parent's ranch-style house on Ann Arbor Road at 6:15pm on a cold Sunday evening on the first of February, waiting to be picked up for Rob's band practice just as I had agreed. Since neither Rob nor I had driver's licenses, he had asked one of the drummers, Tom Masterson, to give us a lift to Veteran's Stadium. My parents were at a Marriage Encounter meeting and my younger sister Leanne and little brother Darren were also gone. I was getting tired of sitting in my room staring at the bubbles of my ten gallon fish tank and looked forward to getting out of the empty house, even though it was just to go watch Rob's silly band practice.

It was a cloudy night with no wind which, from my experience in high school band, made for good marching conditions as long as it didn't start raining. Rob had explained that LBJCB practiced on Tuesday, Thursday and Sunday nights from 6:30 to 9:00pm. Tuesdays and Sunday's were at Vet's Stadium, and Thursdays were at Millikan High School. He told me to be ready on time because if we were late to practice the director, Marvin Marker, would give us plenty of hell about it. It sounded like too much work to me, but I had promised Rob that I would check it out just this once thanks to his brilliant dare. So there I stood in the cold, right on time.

My ears were freezing and I paced up and down the lawn trying to keep warm, but even in my green plaid coat I was shivering. As I paced and waited for my ride, I thought about my day at school which had been a drag. It was my sophomore year at Lakewood High and even though I had transferred from St. Anthony's in hopes of improving both my grades and my social life, I was still just a misfit with a low GPA. I didn't fit in any better than I had at St. Anthony's the year before. *Once a loner, always a loner,* I thought. Most of the cool guys at school fit into either the 'sporto-jock' or the 'surfer-stoner' category and got all the girls, but I was just a 'bando-geek' as they called the people in marching band. This was just another way of calling you a 'nerd' or a 'freak,' which is why I had no interest in hanging out around the band room with those freaky-nerdy-bando-geeks, no way in hell! *And here I am about to meet more bandos thanks to my good 'ole buddy Rob,* I thought, wondering if I was making a colossal mistake by agreeing to go. *Maybe I'll try to get into a rock band...yeah, rock musicians are way more cool than marching bandos!*

My daydream was interrupted by a car screaming around the corner of Lakewood Drive, fishtailing and startling the hell out of me. It was a super clean 1965 white Ford Mustang and I could see the outline of three guys sitting in it. *That's them,* I thought even though I couldn't believe my eyes looking at that bitchin' car. The Mustang came jamming straight up the street, pulled up to the curb in front of me, and stopped sharp with a chirp.

I walked up to the car and the door swung open and scraped against the curb. A real skinny kid with short black hair and the whitest skin I'd ever seen stepped out of the passenger side of the car and pulled his seat forward so I could climb in the back. He had on the same brown and gold sweatshirt as Rob, only his read, 'Cymbals— LBJCB' on the back. As I bent down to get into the back seat I said, "How's it going?" but he only responded with a quick nod.

Rob was sitting in the back on the other side, and I plopped down next to him. "Hey Bri!" he said and pointed to the white-skinned kid, "that's Wally Masterson, and that's his brother Tom." Tom had the same black hair as Wally, but he looked stockier. He had thick sideburns and a dimpled chin just like Dudley Doo-right. "Tom plays snare drum," Rob continued, "and Wally plays the cymbals." Tom was also wearing a drummer sweatshirt with the sleeves cut off at the elbows, just like Robs.

With his hand still on the steering wheel, Tom turned his head toward me but I couldn't see his eyes behind the wire rim sunglasses. He seemed to be studying me and then said, "Hey, how's it going man?" in an intense voice, kinda like Clint Eastwood.

"Hey," I said in response with a quick wave of my hand in the air, trying not to look like a complete nerd.

Once inside the car Wally tugged on the door, but it was stuck in the grass from the extra weight. Tom pulled forward slowly while Wally tried pulling on the door, but it wouldn't shut. It just scraped along the curb, making an awful screeching sound. "Come on Wally, shut the damn door!" Tom snapped back, as if it was Wally's fault that the door wouldn't shut. The car pulled further away from the curb until the door finally came free and slammed shut. Tom was shaking his head as we blazed off toward Vet's Stadium.

No one talked in the car as we headed down Carson Street towards the stadium. The car had an old upholstery smell mixed with cheap mens after-shave. Finally Rob broke the silence, "Hey Tom, you feelin' ready for the Shrine show?"

Rob had previously explained to me that the Shrine show was the next big band performance coming up at the Shrine auditorium in Los Angeles. They had been rehearsing for weeks just to get ready for this show. Since it was 1976, the 'Bi-centennial' year, the show was to be a tribute to all of the old patriotic songs of America, performed on stage by several marching bands. Tom didn't say anything at first. Finally, just as the silence was getting a little uncomfortable, he blurted out, "Yeah, but it'll probably be my last show with the band. If the pageantry girls don't start paying more attention to me, I'm quitting!" I looked at Rob and he just shrugged and smiled. Wally started to giggle, and he had the strangest kind of laugh, starting out slowly, "Huh-huh...huh-huh..." and then building up speed like a motor, "Huh-huh-huh-huh..." It was the weirdest laugh I'd ever heard. I thought, *Who are these guys?*

We pulled into Vet's stadium and sure enough there was the whole scene that Rob had once described to me. It was like the traveling circus setting up for 'The Greatest Show on Earth!' Two huge equipment trucks, painted brightly in red, white, and blue, were parked along the chain link fence in the stadium parking lot. A dozen people in red jackets with 'LBJCB STAFF' stitched on the back worked to unload just about every piece of marching band equipment you could imagine: Shiny brass tubas and marching bells, multi-colored tall flags, a banner on wheels displaying the band name & logo, all came rolling down the ramps. A baton twirler was practicing some amazing maneuvers in a corner near the trucks. Several band members were blowing noisily into their instruments, tuning and warming up as they began to line up in several rows, slowly forming the familiar arrangement of marching ranks and columns. I figured this band must be at least three times the size of the Lakewood High School band.

Tom parked his Mustang next to a lineup of muscle cars that made the parking lot look more like Lion's drag strip. "Oh man, check it out," I whispered to Rob, "look at that orange Dart." It was the cleanest '69 I'd ever seen. It was painted competition orange with a black stripe wrapping around the rear trunk lid from fender to fender...jacked-up in back, and polished chrome rims all around. "That's totally cool," I said, as I stepped out of the Mustang.

"Those are all Drummer cars," Rob said proudly, gazing at the sleek row of hot rods, "they park 'em according to seniority. The Dart belongs to Karl Harkey, he's a tenor drummer. The yellow Olds Cutlass next to it is Greg Golson's. He's also a tenor drummer."

I couldn't believe my eyes. These were the most bitchin' dream cars I'd ever seen up close instead of just in the pages of a Hot Rod magazine.

"The brown '69 Chevy Nova," Rob continued, "that one belongs to Gary Erbe. He plays the bass drum. He waited a long time to get the Nova with the drummer colors." Rob pointed out the detail in the paint job, "See, brown with gold pin-striping, so that he can tell everyone that his is the only custom drummer street rod around."

"Next to that is Gregg Sciotto's car," Rob said, and I could see that it was a stock 1970 Chevy Camaro, canary yellow with chrome Crager rims. It was just like the 1:18 scale AMT car model that I had built a couple of years ago, back when I was into building plastic cars and displaying them on my bedroom shelves. *Second generation Camaro,* I thought, knowing every line of that car. Its only flaw was the maroon rust primer spots all over it. It looked wicked though, like a leopard on the prowl, ready to attack. "We call it the bruised banana," Rob explained, and I chuckled at that one since it wasn't what I was picturing at all. "that car's the fastest one of all the drummer cars, but don't tell a Masterson brother that. Their Dad is a Ford guy...the whole Masterson family is into Fords, and they'll argue it to the death if you even try to tell them that a Chevy is faster than a Ford."

"It's fast as hell though," Rob continued, "trust me, Gregg will take you for a ride in it, and he pulls up to a stop light and then puts a five-dollar bill right on the dashboard. Then he tells you to try to grab the money and he hits the gas," Rob said excitedly, "but so far not one guy has been able to reach the money because that damn car takes off so fast!" Rob motioned in the air like he was shifting Gregg's car into first gear and flooring it. "It slams you back into the seat so hard that you can't fricking move! It's so cool!"

"Wow," I said, trying to hide my enthusiasm. I couldn't believe what I was seeing and hearing about the drummer cars and especially this Gregg guy. I mean, I thought they would all be a bunch of geeks riding their bicycles to band practice like the bandos at school, or driving their parent's jalopies and thinking that was cool. I took another glance across the polished hoods of the drummer cars and realized that I was the geek, not them. I told myself that someday I would get a job so that I could buy a boss Camaro like Gregg's. Just then I noticed another car pulling up at the end of the lineup of drummer cars. It was a white 1967 Dodge Coronet 2-door, stock engine judged by the way it purred, and it had a whip CB antenna arching over the top. I was surprised to hear what sounded like classical music coming from the car. The car stopped and the drivers-side door swung open. A guy with short wavy brown hair, pale skin and freckles got out. He was tall and slim, wearing a white t-shirt, brown Levi's cords, black Converse All-Star tennis shoes, and wire-rimmed sunglasses that hid his eyes. He stretched and looked around, and then in one organized motion he took off the glasses, unfolded his drummer sweatshirt, and pulled it over his head. He put the glasses back on and pulled a yellow baseball cap from his back pocket. Positioning it onto his head, he leveled the brim perfectly over his eyes, and I couldn't help but think that he looked like General MacArthur stepping out of a military jeep, preparing to address his troops.

He walked around to the other side of the car to open the passenger door, and out stepped the most beautiful red headed female I'd ever seen. She wore red Vans sneakers, white shorts revealing perfectly shaped legs, and a gold sweatshirt with the name 'Lynn' embroidered on the front. She stepped away from the car and waved to some other girls across the way, as the drummer locked and shut the car door behind her. *Wow, being a drummer in this band sure has its advantages,* I thought, once again amazed at how wrong I was about these guys. I knew that I must be witnessing drummer royalty as they gracefully walked towards us, he with a pair of snare drumsticks in one hand and she holding his other hand.

"Who are they?" I asked Rob.

"That's Dave Geopforth and his girlfriend Lynn Austin," he replied. "he plays snare drum and she's the lead pageantry girl. He's been in a couple of years, since '74. Word is he'll be voted as head drummer since Lonny will be stepping down soon."

As Dave and Lynn walked past us, Dave looked at Tom and smiled, and then shook his hand as well as Rob's and Wally's. It wasn't a regular handshake, but the 'soul brother' kind where the hands come up and connect at an angle. "Hey Dave, this is my friend Brian," Rob said, pointing at me. "he's never seen us, but he came down to check us out."

Dave reached out his hand, and imitating what I'd just seen, I shook his hand in the same way. "Pleasure," he said, and I nodded in return, noticing the reflection of my goofy face in his mirrored glasses. As he and Lynn continued on towards the band trucks, Lynn looked at me and smiled and I melted over the most pretty smile and white teeth I'd ever laid eyes on. I'm sure I grinned back like a dufus, with drool coming out of my mouth. She smelled so good too…it was an intoxicating mix of Charley perfume, fruity LipSmackers lip-gloss, and spearmint chewing gum. *Every pretty girl must smell like that,* I thought, and made a silent vow to make every effort to get closer to that scent.

I followed Rob and the other two guys to the band trucks, and we walked up to a cluster of guys all wearing drummer sweatshirts. They were talking and laughing and it looked like they were waiting for one of the trucks to be opened. When they saw us they started exchanging the same 'drummer' handshake and Rob introduced me to each guy one at a time. I felt nervous and awkward meeting new people as I always did, but these guys seemed pretty cool so far.

"Three, Please!" shouted one of the drummers as a band staff member unlocked the rear door of the equipment truck and swung it open. The staff member climbed up into the truck and started untying rope and then pulling down canvas bags shaped like drums. Unzipping the first black vinyl bag, the man produced a red-sparkle Ludwig snare drum, with polished chrome rims and yellow cord criss-crossing around it. *Kind of like their muscle cars,* I thought with amusement, as I stared at the perfectly polished drum, the street lights reflecting beautifully off of the deep red metal-flake. The drummer took it and quickly hooked it to the white cloth drum strap slung over his shoulder, then adjusted it so that it rested comfortably just above the left knee.

"Every drummer is given his own drum and they're numbered," Rob explained to me, as the next guy in line called out his number. I watched as more snare, tenor, and bass drums were pulled out from their black bags, as well as several shiny pairs of brass cymbals. Then a guy with a snare drum took five steps away from the truck, raised his wooden drumsticks high over his head, and with an angry look he came down hard on the drum. RAT-TAT-TAT-TAT-TAT-TAT-TAT-TAT!

I jumped back in shock, the sound exploding in my ears like a machine gun. "Holy Shit!" I said and looked at Rob who saw my reaction and started laughing. "That's the loudest damn drum I've ever heard," I said, covering my ears with my hands.

"Sorry bro, I should've warned you," Rob said, but I knew this was just BS because Rob was always figuring out ways to shake me up. "Stand by," he continued, "because believe me, that was nothing. The guys are just tuning up." I looked at all of the drummers getting ready and tried to imagine what they would sound like when they all played at once.

Rob was the last guy to get his drum from the truck and join the rest of them. The drummers were scattered around the parking lot and pounding on their drums so loud that I had to keep my hands over my ears. They weren't playing together yet, so the sound was just earsplitting and chaotic. One of the drummers was stooped over his bass drum, and leaning it almost flat to the ground, he pounded down on the wide drumhead with his mallet with the same angry face as the snare drummer. BOOM-BOOM-BOOM-BOOM-BOOM! It sounded like the cannon of a gunship. There were cymbal players twirling their cymbals in the air with a flash of golden brass, then bringing them together hard, creating a loud "CHICK!" sound. A tenor drummer swung both of his arms up and down over his head, coming down so hard on the drum that it sounded like a shotgun firing off. BLAM-BLAM-BLAM-BLAM-BLAM! The tone of the some of the drums actually did drop after a few beats with the sticks and mallets, and guys were using a metal drum key shaped like a 'T' to tighten up the lugs of the drumheads. I laughed to myself, thinking of how Rob called this violent pounding 'tuning' as if you could call it anything musical, putting it in the same category as a violin player fine-tuning his strings!

I was really impressed with the size of the drum section as I counted a total of nine snare drummers, seven tenors, five bass drummers, and six cymbal players. Some guys looked about age twelve or thirteen, and others looked older, maybe nineteen or twenty. They all had short hair and the older guys had long side burns. *No chick drummers though,* I thought, and wondered if there was some kind of rule about this, because we sure had girl drummers in our high school band.

I watched the tenor and bass drummers wrapping white first-aid tape around each finger, and then put a pair of cloth gloves over that, followed by a pair of leather gloves. *Three layers!* I thought, and wondered why they needed so much protection. They looked more ready for a boxing match than a band practice. Finally they took a heavy-duty drum mallet in each gloved hand and tied the thick nylon chord attached to each metal shaft around their fingers. I figured that this must be to keep the mallets from flying out of their hands when they played.

Suddenly there were three sharp blasts of a whistle and someone shouted, "FALL INTO POSITION!" I turned around and saw a short, stocky man with jet-black hair standing next to a red station wagon. He was wearing a red windbreaker and held a clipboard in one hand and a megaphone in the other. Rob walked up to me with his drum in hand and his snare sticks protruding from his armpit. "That's the band director, Marvin Marker," he said, and then walked past me and out towards the band formation. "Gotta go now, its show time!" I watched as Marvin took full command of the group.

"Masterson, Oakley...get into position!" he shouted, as band members scrambled with their instruments to find their places in the marching ranks that were forming. This was a much bigger marching band than my high school band, and I figured there must be over a hundred members. Up front two pageantry girls rolled the 'LBJCB' banner into place, and behind them was the baton twirler, who was practicing throwing the baton high into the air and catching it. A dozen pageantry girls followed holding eight-foot tall colored flags that formed a large 'V' and the drum major stood behind them. Planting the tip of the drum major baton (or 'mace' as Rob called it) firmly on the ground, the drum major marked the imaginary line for the front rank of trombone players to line up. *Wow, seven columns across, going fourteen ranks back,* I thought as a full-fledged marching band materialized before my eyes. I saw the drummers lining up in the very back and there was one more rank of pageantry girls with tall flags standing behind them.

When the last of the band members found their places, everyone stood perfectly still with their heads pointing downward, waiting for the next command. You could hear a pin drop as the clouds rolled over the McDonnell Douglas Aircraft hangars to the west, a fresh breeze bringing on an evening chill. I was amazed at their discipline and concentration and thought of how different this was from my high school band, where people just goofed off during practice. Finally I heard the click of a megaphone and Marvin spoke into it, "Okay Jeff, you can start when you're ready." The drum major nodded and lifted his mace.

"BAND! A-TENNN-HUT!" he barked and the drummers sounded off in unison with a thunderous ROLL-BOOM! The whole group brought their heads up and snapped their legs together in a split second, shouting "RAH!" The drummers held their arms up, crossing their drumsticks directly in front of their stony faces. They were as still as toy soldiers. There were four ranks of drummers lined up in the order of snare line first, then tenors, then bass drums and finally cymbals. I noticed that some of the drummers had gold stripes sewn onto the left sleeve of their sweatshirts. I guessed that the stripes indicated the number of years that the guy had been in the drum section because the head drummer Lonny had six stripes, but Rob only had one. I also noticed that the senior drummers marched on the right side while the guys with less seniority marched on the left. Lonny had the right-guide position in the front rank of seven snare drummers, with Dave Geopforth in the center, and Rob on the very left closest to where I was standing.

The drum major shouted "Rim-beat!" and stepped-off the band with four quick chirps of his whistle, "Tweet-Tweet-Tweet-Tweet!" With that every left foot lifted and stepped forward, and the drummers began playing a rumbling low-volume drum beat in perfect rhythm as the band began to march. Bu-dum-bum(chee)-bum(chee)-bum(chee)-bum, bu-dum-bum(chee)-bum(chee)-bum...

The band moved forward with graceful strides like one big teen-army, and I walked in step along side of them, completely forgetting that I had been freezing in the evening air just a minute ago. As the drummers played the rim beat something inside of me churned.

Wow, what a bitchin' sound. I thought, as I watched the drummers swinging their red-sparkle drums majestically in unison, their mallets and sticks moving up and down in perfect syncopated rhythm. This was no tri-tom tapping, high-tension snare drum pattering rudimental style of playing, no way. These guys laid out a simpler, slower four-four count cadence, the kind that got right into your bloodstream. If the band were a Roman army, then the drummers were most certainly the gladiators, the way they commenced forward with such seriousness. They reminded me of foot soldiers going into battle, sounding off the war cry with every pulsating beat of their drums.

Then I saw a motion from the head drummer Lonny, as he lifted his left arm high in the air with a hand signal. I figured this must be to indicate the next drum cadence and it gave me an adrenaline rush just to see it. My heart raced as the hand signal was silently relayed down the snare line for the rest of the drummers, and then the rim beat finished and they clicked off four more beats leading into the next cadence.

What I heard next was like M60 machine guns going off and Howitzer war cannons exploding, with me caught in the crossfire! The bass drummers lifted their arms straight out in unison and swung down so hard with their mallets that the asphalt shook under my feet. BOOM-BA-BOOM-BOOM… TA-TA-TA-TA-TA-TA-TA-TA… BOOM-BA-BOOM-BOOM… TA-TA-TA-TA-BAM-BAM-BAM-BAM!! The rest of the drummers raised their arms high overhead in turn, contorting their faces and playing the cadence as loud as they could with every strand of every muscle in their bodies. The snare drummers thrashed and the tenors pounded away, giving it everything they had.

It was controlled violence in motion, with a deafening sound, yet it wasn't sloppy. They created precise rhythmic layers of percussion and it was as if every rank of snare, tenor and bass drummers were challenging each other back and forth, communicating in some kind of primordial language. The cymbal players crashed their cymbals in flawless accents outward towards the sky, creating shimmering arches of brass overhead. I stood on the sidelines with my mouth hanging open, totally astonished. *Oh...my...God.* I thought in total amazement, not believing my eyes or ears. Never before in my life had I seen or heard anything so awesome!

Lonny held up another hand signal and the drummers seamlessly clicked right into the next cadence. They hammered down on those drums violently as they marched forward, and one of them screamed, "Come on you Wussies, PLAY!" They were sweating and thrashing and grunting, and I mean they were balls-to-the-wall WAILING! The thunderous beat of the cadences pierced my body and echoed out across the horizon, bouncing off of the foothills and straight up to the gods. Never before had anything spoken so directly to my soul. I watched these guys play drums until their hands bled and their bodies trembled with fatigue and something stirred so deeply inside of me that *I wanted to cry in that moment.* I had a sick sense that Rob had been right all along... I had been missing out on something, big time.

The drum major marched in front swinging his mace up and down, and then he raised his other arm with a hand signal. The band members immediately lifted their instruments in ready position to begin the first song of the night. Someone yelled, "It's Cal Poly fanfare!" and Lonny relayed the hand signal back to the drummers. The cadence ended abruptly, and there was a three-count silence just before the brass horns blew the first notes of Cal Poly. I smiled as I heard the last beat of the drum cadence ring out to the sky, ricochet off of the stadium walls, and then trail away into oblivion like a phantom... all within that silence.

I want in, I thought, with more yearning than I could hardly stand. *I want to trade in my stupid skateboard for a pair of drumsticks and a brown & gold sweatshirt!* From that moment on, I knew that I'd do whatever they said or go through whatever it took, including selling my soul, to become one of them.

CHAPTER 3

The Long Beach Junior Concert Band marched into the night, rehearsing songs and practicing whatever street maneuver the drum major commanded, including left turns, right flanks, step-offs and halts. The pageantry girls went over their flag routines, while the drummers pounded out more cadences in a grueling marathon, blasting their drumbeats out to the streets of Long Beach. It made me grin to think of how the sound must be broadcasting across the dinner tables of all the residents within a five mile radius. I expected the cops to show up any minute to give the drum section a ticket for disturbing the peace.

If I didn't get to Rob right away to ask him how to go about joining the drum section, I knew that I would just bust. I anxiously waited for my chance, but the band kept on going, marching for another half hour and then lining up in a 'stage' formation to practice for the Shrine show. The band rehearsed several patriotic tunes and practiced a side-stepping motion, splitting in half while the pageantry girls marched up the middle and formed a high-kicking chorus line. Marvin Marker paced back and forth nervously, shouting directions into his megaphone and saying, "From the top, do it again!" until the band members were moaning and groaning. The drummers even got to play a set of cadences as part of the show, Marvin calling it the 'drum feature.' I watched as the drum section practiced marching straight out to the edge of the imaginary stage, planted their feet, and then hit the audience with three solid minutes of the loudest cadences they could play. Rob told me that the drummers always got a standing ovation at the Shrine show, which didn't surprise me one bit after what I had seen so far!

As the band finished rehearsing the last two songs, 'America the Beautiful' and 'This is My Country,' staff members rolled out two big plastic floats in front of the band, one shaped like a bald eagle sitting atop a globe and the other shaped like Uncle Sam's top hat. Both lit up right on cue with the music, the brilliantly colored light bulbs flashing as the final dramatic notes of the 'grand finale' were played. It was around nine o'clock by the time Marvin finally called out, "Last run through!" and everyone cheered in relief. The band went through the whole show one more time, and when the last song finished everyone stood at attention, waiting to be dismissed.

After a couple of minutes of silence, Marvin clicked on the megaphone once again and said, "Good job tonight folks...just a few announcements before we wrap up." I could hear more groans coming from the band members. "Quiet please," Marvin said with an impatient tone.

I remembered that Rob had told me this was the worst part of band practice. "You're standing in the freezing cold, so tired you're ready to fricking collapse," he told me, "and Marvin has to go through his list of 'announcements!' Jeez, what does he think man, that we're in the Army or something?"

Sure enough, Marvin started talking through the megaphone, reading from his clipboard. "All band uniforms must be cleaned and pressed before show time," he droned on, "everyone must be on the buses at no later than ten o'clock that morning..." Even the adult staff members looked tired and ready to go home as they paced back and forth trying to keep warm. I was also hopping up and down from the cold night air, and even though steam was coming off of the shoulders of the sweaty drummers, I thought they must be cooling off fast and feeling it too. The band members looked very tired from the long rehearsal, yet they stood in place like real troopers, and I had to respect their level of dedication and self-control.

Marvin continued talking, going on about this thing he called 'OBST,' short for 'our band sticks together,' and how teamwork was important and every band member needed to do their part to make the Shrine show the best one yet. Even though I kind of liked what he was saying, it was obvious that he had lost his audience, because the band members and staff were fidgeting and murmuring, looking like they just wanted to pack it up and go home.

Finally Marvin said, "That's about it for tonight. Tuesday practice is cancelled, but we'll see you at six-thirty sharp on Thursday, at Millikan field." He then gave the drum major the go-ahead to dismiss the band. The drum major turned towards the band and waited for everyone to quiet down in the 'at ease' position. When all was silent to his satisfaction, he took in a deep breath and shouted "BAND, A-TENNN-HUT!" and the band snapped their legs together with their heads up one last time. He then shouted "BAND, DIS-MISSED!" and the whole group did an immediate 'about face,' shouted "STEP-TURN-BOOM!" in response, and then scattered out like ants towards the equipment trucks and their cars to make their way home.

People were lined up around the trucks talking and waiting to turn in their instruments as several of the LBJCB staff worked quickly to load everything from tubas to flags to the bulky plastic floats. The stadium parking lot was clearing out, as people got into their own cars or waited for their parents to pick them up late on a school night. The only people not leaving were the drummers. They stood in place right where the drum major had dismissed the band, with their sticks still crossed at their faces, and not moving a muscle. *What the hell are they doing now?* I thought, and walked over to where Rob was standing.

Lonny stepped away from his right guide position and faced the drummers. Lonny Daquiado was dark skinned with black hair, a stocky build, and a serious look that reminded me of Charles Bronson in 'Death Wish.' He stood quietly in the light of the parking lot lamps, his drummer sweatshirt damp with sweat, and twirled a drumstick with his right hand every few seconds, as if it helped him to think. The drummers stood still 'at attention,' waiting for his next words. Even though there were cars rolling by and the bustle of the band still clearing out of the parking lot, Lonny seemed oblivious. A couple of minutes went by before he finally spoke, and his words were calm and to the point.

"Drummers, we still have a tryout tonight," he said, and I realized that the drummers were not done yet. "It is Mark McMullen's fifth tryout on snare drum, and I need to have as many of you hang around as possible so that we can vote on him." Lonny paced back and forth, pointing his drumstick at each guy as he spoke their names. "Sam, Karl, Wally...you three stay to play for the tryout," He continued, "Mark, you stay put at attention until we're ready...and I need the rest of you to sack 'em up and get back here ASAP so we can start." A cold breeze hit the back of my neck and although I was still freezing, I shrugged it off because I couldn't wait to see what happened next. "Make it quick boys and we'll get this done and get out of here," Lonny said, and he stepped back into place in the snare drum rank, brought himself to attention with his sticks crossed, and stood silently. After a few seconds he yelled, "Drummers, DIS-MISSED!"

Every drummer except Mark, Sam, Karl and Wally turned and shouted, "STEP-TURN-BOOM!" and headed for the equipment trucks. Mark McMullen stood staring straight ahead with his sticks crossed, waiting for his fifth chance to become a drummer. He was shorter like me, maybe five foot eight, with a muscular build, short brown hair, and sharp blue eyes. He did not say a word nor move a muscle and, judged by the determined look on his face, he was dead serious about this tryout. I couldn't believe how involved it was, having to try out so many times just to get into this drum section. *Jeez, in high school band all you had to do was memorize some basic drum beats and they gave you a uniform,* I thought.

"BAH!!" Rob yelled into my ear from behind, startling the hell out of me.

"Damn it, Rob!" I said, and pushed him back, but instantly regretted touching his wet sweatshirt. He had put his drum away and was the first guy back from the trucks.

"So, you liked the drums, didn't ya?" he asked excitedly, as if reading my mind. "Come on tell me Bri, wha'd ya think?!" I'm sure he could see the answer written all over my face.

"What can I say dude," I replied, "I admit it, you were right...just tell me what I need to do, and sign me the hell up!"

"Bitchin,' dude!" Rob said with a look of supreme satisfaction. "We'll talk to Lonny right after the tryout." Rob turned his attention towards the trainee standing before us. "Mark here goes to Los Alamitos High, same as

Geopforth," He continued, "Mark and Dave are buds and Dave recruited him," Rob picked at a blister on his hand as he spoke, and I noticed salty streaks of sweat down the side of his face. "I heard that Mark lives with his Mom and brother in Seal Beach. Mark is already part of the drum section, but he's a cymbal player. He wants to get in on snare drum." Rob continued, "A cymbal player isn't considered a 'real drummer' until he gets voted in on snare, tenor, or bass drum. Even though the cymbal players march with the drummers, they wear a different sweatshirt." As Rob explained this, I remembered that Wally's sweatshirt did read, 'LBJCB Cymbals,' not 'LBJCB Drummer' like the other guys. "If a cymbal player wants to step up to the drum," he said, "it's like starting all over."

"Wow, I had no idea," I responded, genuinely amazed. "How did Mark learn all of the drum cadences?" I asked.

"Like all trainees," Rob continued, "Mark was assigned a 'big brother,' a senior drummer to teach him every drum cadence, the hand signals, how to march, tune up his drum...everything. His big brother is Bob Coryell, right over there." Rob pointed to a guy that had just walked up to Mark and was pointing at him and talking just like a coach would. "Bobby has been spending weeks helping Mark to get through these tryouts." Rob came in closer to me, his voice now a whisper. "And get this, Mark doesn't even have good rhythm, he gets out of step all the time and keeps screwing up the cadences, but he's got guts and a lot of heart, which is mostly what we're looking for in a drummer." I was impressed to hear that guys with no musical background like Mark actually had a shot at being in a band like LBJCB if they worked hard enough to learn the drum. "We keep voting him out," Rob continued, "but he won't give up, he keeps coming back for more!"

I felt real nervous for Mark as he stood there with a red sparkle drum slung to his knee. The drum looked too big on him all of a sudden. With Sam, Karl and Wally spreading out behind him and the other twenty drummers surrounding him in the front, he looked like he was about to be fed to the lions!

I whispered to Rob, "Catch you later," and walked over to the chain-link fence that surrounded the parking lot. I wanted to be far enough away from the drummers not to be noticed, but still close enough to watch all of the action.

I could see that the parking lot had cleared out almost completely, except for a handful of drummer girlfriends huddled near the drummer cars and one equipment truck with a single staff member waiting, having gotten the unlucky task of hanging around until the drummers finished. The breeze had stopped and a thick mist was forming in the night air, creating beads of moisture in my hair and floating through the beams of the streetlamps like spirits passing through. This gave the parking lot an eerie feeling, and the drummer tryout took on a mystical quality, like some kind of tribal religious ceremony was about to take place.

The drummers were spread out in front of Mark, waiting for Lonny to begin the tryout. Some of them were standing, some were sitting, and some actually lit up cigarettes and were pacing back and forth as they waited. No one talked much, probably because they were tired or just going into some kind of mental mode for the tryout. It was a quirky collection of guys when you studied them standing there with their brown sweatshirts, sideburns, and short hair. If I hadn't seen the way they played drums a few minutes earlier, I'd have thought they were just a bunch of odd looking dudes and nothing more. They were short, tall, fat and skinny, and some of them wore eyeglasses and had acne, and they smelled like the weirdest mix of cheap Avon cologne you could imagine. When they strapped those drums on though, something changed and they became the toughest looking sons-of-bitches I'd ever seen, wailing away like invincible machines! Putting on that brown and gold drummer sweatshirt was like some kind of alter ego for them...they were just band geeks by day, but then hook on a red sparkle drum at night and suddenly you're this confident, cocky bad-ass drummer. The drummers seemed really strange but also totally cool, and the sound of those cadences...man, I desperately wanted to be a part of that.

Finally Lonny walked to the spot directly in front of Mark and faced him. He paused for a moment, stared straight into Mark's eyes, and then held up his pinky finger. "Rimbeat," he said, and then counted off four clicks of his drumsticks to begin the tryout. Mark and the other two drummers lowered their sticks to their drums and started playing the low jungle-beat I had heard during marching practice. Wally came right in on cue with his cymbals, choking them together during the off-beats. Lonny then held out another hand signal, and Mark planted his feet and shifted his body, his face deep in concentration as he prepared to show the drummers what he was made of.

The red snare drum bounced and rocked under the assault of Mark's drumsticks and the sound ricocheted off the asphalt and shot out like a rifle. Even with just four guys playing, the drums were loud and Mark stared straight ahead as he thrashed out every accent of every drum beat he had memorized. The other three guys were amazing to watch. Sam was on bass drum, throwing his mallets out sideways, twirling them in a 'figure-eight' pattern and then hitting the drum so hard that he actually had to swing his lower torso into each punch just to keep his balance. It was like some strange dance he was doing from the waist down. Watching Karl on tenor just blew my mind as he swung his mallets straight up in vertical columns and came down dead center on that drum head every single time. His arm muscles flexed and strained as he played and there was a round pocket forming in the middle of the drumhead that made the drum sound like a shotgun. I thought it could break apart any second, but somehow that Remo drum head held together. I had been playing tenor drum in high school band for the past couple of years, but nothing even came close to this. Wally brought his fifteen-inch brass Zildjians together so hard that I couldn't help but stare at the brass rings of the cymbals, sure that they would start cracking right before my eyes. I had never seen such intensity in a cymbal player before. This was the most awesome style of drum playing I'd ever seen!

Lonny threw out more hand signals and Mark kept playing as the other three backed him up faithfully. Mark seemed to have every hand signal and drum beat memorized and I couldn't detect the goofs that Rob had described earlier. After the first half a dozen cadences he started to grit his teeth with fatigue, and the drummers seemed to love this, cheering, "Come-on McMullen, play you bastard!" Mark spit and gasped for air, but kept thrashing his sticks down on the drum while Lonny threw out more hand signals. It all seemed kind of cruel in a way and yet, after watching how hard they played, I understood the necessity of testing the strength and ability of a trainee and realized that this style of drumming was not for everyone...not for weaklings.

The moment of truth was bearing down hard on Mark, but he would not give up. He played every cadence as loud as he could, even though his whole body was shaking with exhaustion. At one point a drumstick flew out of his hand, but one of the drummers quickly reached down and grabbed it, and handed it back to him in a simple gesture of support. That right there told me that these guys liked him and would probably vote him into the drum section tonight. All four guys were flailing and grunting and dripping with sweat. By now the other drummers were in a frenzy, jumping up and down and screaming, "YEEE-HAAA MARK... Wail! Go-Go-Go...!" I got totally caught up in the excitement, whispering to myself, *Go Mark, don't give up!* as he strained and suffered, holding his own, but looking ready to collapse. Lonny finally lifted a drumstick and swiped it across his neck to indicate 'Stop.'

When they finished the cadence they brought their feet together and their arms up with sticks crossed at attention. The last beat of the cadence echoed out to the sky, dissolving into crisp, cold silence. Mark could barely hold his arms up and you could see his chest heaving in and out, gasping for air. Lonny mercifully said, "Drummers, AT-EASE!" and they dropped their arms and heads down. "Good job guys. You four can sack 'em up. Mark, you wait by the truck... Sam and Karl, get back here so we can vote." Lonny waved his arm and pointed his drumstick toward the truck. "Go!"

Mark hobbled over to the truck, sacked his drum, and then stood leaning over with his hands on his knees, still catching his breath. Wally was placing his cymbals in a round vinyl bag while Sam and Karl also sacked their drums and then ran back to join the huddle of drummers. They stood in a tight circle with Lonny in the center and I couldn't hear a word they said from my spot by the fence, only their murmuring and an occasional burst of laughter. From what Rob had told me though, I knew they were giving Mark either a thumbs-up or a thumbs-down. "We take turns saying what we like or don't like about the guy," Rob had explained, "his drum playing, strength, attitude...and then we take a vote. You only need a majority vote to get in, so one guy can make the difference if there is an even split. There's always some wise-ass that waits to vote last, but Lonny keeps things pretty fair."

In less than five minutes the drummers broke the huddle with a clap of hands and the vote was done. Mark's big brother Bob walked up to him and put a hand on his shoulder, no doubt giving him the news. I was dying to find out if he'd made it or not, but I couldn't tell by their faces if the news was good or bad. Just then Rob walked in front of me and blocked my view and, just as I was about to make a snide remark, I saw that Lonny was standing right next to him. "Brian McBride?" Lonny asked, and held out his hand.

"Yeah...hey Lonny," I replied, feeling self-conscious all of a sudden. Rob had wasted no time telling Lonny that I was interested. I grasped his hand and we exchanged the drummer handshake. Lonny's hand felt leathery from a thick layer of calluses, built up from years of playing marching snare drum.

"I'm Lonny the head drummer. I see you've already been introduced to the handshake. That's good...let's take a walk."

Lonny led me along the chain link fence surrounding the stadium, and he didn't say a word at first. He looked up towards the sky as if formulating exactly what he would say next. The silence was making me nervous, so I finally cracked and made a feeble attempt to start a conversation. "You guys are really great, man. I mean wow..."

Lonny interrupted as if he hadn't heard me. "So Rob tells me you want to join the drum section. Do you have any experience on drums?" he asked, and I knew he wanted to get right down to business.

"Yes, I was in Saint Anthony's band for a year, and now I'm in Lakewood high band."

Lonny nodded favorably, and then said, "That's good. What did you have in mind...cymbals maybe, or a go at snare drum? We really need snare drummers, and you're about the right size I'd say."

At that moment it became crystal clear what drum I wanted to play the most. I gulped and said, "Well, actually I sorta wanted to play the tenor drum. That's what I play in high school band, and..."

"Oh really?" he said, interrupting me again with a disappointed look on his face. I thought he was going to laugh at me, tell me no way in hell, that I was too small to handle the tenor drum. My heart started to pound in my chest as I realized that if he said no, I might have to insist on tenor drum and risk losing my chance to even be a trainee. I knew what he was thinking, that his tenor drummers were way bigger and stronger than me, all seven of them. I knew he was right, that I would have to build muscle on my skinny arms and it would be the biggest challenge of my whole life...but I didn't care, because tenor drum was the only choice. Even though we used cheap hollow tenor mallets in high school band and didn't play nearly as hard, I was drawn to tenor drum from the very beginning because to me it was the hardest drum to play, and the heart of the whole cadence!

Lonny didn't say a word for an excruciatingly long minute, no doubt contemplating how to respond to my request. He finally turned to me and said, "Well if it's tenor drum you want... I'll give you a shot at it, but here's the deal...if it doesn't work out, I'm putting you on snare drum. Fair enough?"

I nodded my head with a grin, totally relieved. "That's great, that's just great!" I said, both thrilled and frightened at the same time. "Thanks Lonny, I promise I'll practice and do my best to..."

Lonny cut me off again, no more interested in my blubbering than before. "I'm assigning Jeff O'Keefe as your big brother. He's been in for about a year, and he's pretty good. He'll teach you everything you need to know for your first tryout." Lonny stopped abruptly, then turned around and started walking back towards the drummers and I followed. "Let's go back and you can meet him. Congratulations, Brian. You are now officially a drummer trainee. You've got a lot of work ahead of you."

As we walked back to the drummers, I couldn't stop smiling I was so stoked. It seemed like my whole life was changing in a single night. I couldn't believe how I had resisted Rob all this time. Sure he had steered me wrong in the past with the karate lessons that almost killed me and the ice skating disaster...but what a dickhead I was for not taking his word for it this time. Before the band practice I didn't know squat about these drummers and now all I wanted to do was be an LBJCB drummer! I was more excited than ever and at the same time scared shitless. This was totally unlike me...way beyond my comfort zone. I pictured myself standing up there for a tryout, with all those guys watching me, and I could already feel the panic. I'd either pull it off on tenor drum, or make a total jackass of myself. *But it's worth it!* I thought, taking a chance for the first time in my life. I didn't know what was going to happen next, all I knew was that this was the most awesome drum section I had ever seen or heard, and that somehow I *should* be in it! I'd never felt like that about anything before. I just hoped to God that this guy Jeff knew his stuff and could show me the way.

Lonny and I walked up to the drummers, who were all standing around Mark slapping him on the back and shaking his hand. Mark had a shit-eating grin on his face and I knew that he had been voted in. "See you at the next practice Brian," Lonny said, "Thursday, Millikan High School, six-thirty sharp. We'll get you set up with a tenor drum." He shook my hand again and walked over to Mark to congratulate him. Rob spotted me and walked over.

"Mark got voted in!" he said, "Can you believe it, five fricking tryouts but he finally did it! I knew he could do it. Hey, how'd it go for you?"

"Great... I'm starting Thursday night as a trainee," I said, and Rob slapped my shoulder.

"Bitchin dude...which drum?" I looked at him like he should know better.

"What do you think, man? Tenor drum of course!" I replied.

Rob looked genuinely surprised. "Tenor! Shit, talk about stepping up with the big boys. Ballsy move Bri...who's your big bro?" he asked, and I had to think for second to remember the name.

"Guy named Jeff."

"Jeff O'Keefe?" Rob said slowly, nodding with approval. "He's an animal on tenor...a real powerhouse. That's cool man! He'll show you the ropes. Come on over so you can meet him." We walked over to the drummers and Rob yelled, "Jeff!" A big Hawaiian-looking dude who must have been at least six feet tall and two hundred pounds turned and walked toward us. "Jeff, this is my friend Brian," Rob said, "he's the guy I said was coming tonight to watch us."

Rob stepped aside as Jeff walked up, and Jeff sized me up and then looked back at Rob. "Brian, meet Jeff," Rob said before Jeff could say anything.

Jeff shook my hand and said, "What's up dude?" His hands had the same leathery pads as Lonny's.

Rob said, "Brian wants to learn tenor drum and Lonny made you his big brother."

"No shit Sherlock, Lonny just told me," Jeff said, and it didn't sound too encouraging. He took another look at me and then said, "I guess anything's possible."

Before I could say anything Rob jumped in, "Hey bro, give the guy a chance. Bri here has been in high school band for almost two years now...and on tenor drum. He'll be great!" Jeff's face relaxed a little with this information. I figured he was thinking that at least he wouldn't be starting from scratch with me. I couldn't wait for the chance to show Jeff that I could actually march and play a tenor drum.

"Cool. We'll see how it goes." Jeff said in a more accepting tone. "Meet me at practice an hour early on Thursday and I'll start teaching you some cadences. You got a car?"

"Nope, not yet," I replied with a shrug.

"Too bad, cuz I was going to bum a ride off you." he said, cracking a smile that revealed big white teeth against his dark skin. He didn't seem so bad after-all. "No worries, just meet me there at five-thirty." With that Jeff waved a 'hang loose' sign and walked back towards the drummers.

Rob said, "I'll see if Tom can pick us up early on Thursday. We better get going, I see Tom and Wally heading for their car."

The band truck pulled out of the parking lot, leaving only the drummers and their cars under the misty glow of the streetlights. Rob and I walked over to Tom's car and Tom motioned for us to get in. "I can't stay boys. We gotta go." Rob and I climbed into the back seat, and Wally jumped in, slamming the door shut as Tom fired up the Mustang.

We started pulling out of the parking lot and I noticed that we were the only ones leaving. I looked over to the drummers and I couldn't believe my eyes. I rolled down the small triangular rear window of the car to get a better look, and saw Mark McMullen running his ass off with the whole drum section chasing after him. The drummers were yelling, "GET HIM!" and even though Mark was laughing, I could tell that he was trying his damnedest to outrun them.

Tom said, "Hey, check it out," and slowed down the car so we could watch.

Mark got as far as the grass field across from the stadium, but that was a big mistake because it gave the drummers the perfect chance to tackle him. One guy hurled his arms around Mark's ankles and yelled, "Got your ass!" and they both fell forward, skidding on the grass. Mark covered his head with his arms as if he knew exactly what was coming, and sure enough a dozen more guys dog-piled him. They heaped on top of Mark in a jumble of flailing arms and legs, as if he'd just fumbled the ball at the Super Bowl. I could see his shoes sticking out at the bottom of the pile, but the rest of him was totally buried. The drummers were laughing hysterically and yelling "Banzai!" as they took turns jumping on top of the mass of bodies. They had that frantic and crazed look...it was a scene right out of 'Lord of the Flies!' Finally they peeled off of Mark and helped him up, then took turns shaking his hand to congratulate him again. Other than a few grass stains on his clothes he looked okay...in fact, he looked totally psyched-up!

"What the hell is that?" I asked Rob in disbelief, no doubt witnessing yet another aspect of this mysterious new drummer world. Tom and Wally were busting up laughing and Rob had his hands over his face, trying to hide the fact that he had also enjoyed watching Mark getting thoroughly pummeled.

"That's what we do when a new guy gets in the drum section." Rob said, his eyes watering up from laughing. "We call it drummer initiation!"

CHAPTER 4

I sat in my bedroom hunched over my desk after school, staring blankly at the pages of my Geometry book. I couldn't concentrate on homework at all, not after what I had witnessed the night before...not after seeing the LBJCB drummers. Although I tried to concentrate on the math equations in front of me, my head swirled with thoughts of red drums, brown sweatshirts, and pretty pageantry girls. *Nope, can't get a damn thing done tonight,* I thought. My first band practice with LBJCB as a trainee was Thursday night, and they would be giving me a tenor drum and a chance to prove myself. Time was not moving fast enough between Monday and Thursday though and it was driving me nuts. It felt like my head would burst into flames any second from the anticipation. For some reason getting into this drum section was so exciting that the more I tried to push it out of my mind, the more my feet kept stomping out drum beats on the floor!

So there I sat, getting behind in my math homework, while my feet stomped and my hands tapped on the edge of the desk with two pencils. I probably looked like a wind-up toy monkey. *Mellow-out goofball.* I thought, as I set down the pencils and reached for an old shoe box sitting on the shelf over my desk. I opened the lid and admired the prized possessions inside…my Hot Wheels collection and a stack of Odd-Rods trading cards. I grabbed a few of the Odd-Rods cards and flipped through them, chuckling at the familiar images of 'Mad Shifter,' 'Chrome Coffin,' and 'Week-end Warrior.' *Monsters driving hot rods… God I love that!* I thought, and remembered the drummer muscle cars. Setting the cards down I clicked on my AM radio. Turning the knob slowly, I stared at the black vertical line passing over the green AM scale. It was my favorite hobby lately, mining the AM airways for a boss tune. Starting at '530 kHz,' whatever that was, I dialed clockwise all the way over to 1600 kHz, listening to the scratchy static between each station, and hoping to hit on a good song. I passed through the news and weather, a religious channel, and a jazz station, but found nothing good. *I can't wait until I get the AM/FM stereo with built-in 8-track tape player and speakers for my birthday…then I can play what I want, when I want it.* I thought, realizing that August 15th was still six months away. I had begged my parents for a new stereo, promising that this was ALL that I wanted for my birthday, and explaining that my record player was busted and this AM clock radio just wasn't cutting it anymore, so I really, really needed it. *Oh well, this will have to do for now,* I thought and kept dialing, this time counterclockwise, and tuned it all the way to 930 KHJ which was broadcasting a Carpenters song. *Too mellow,* I thought and continued a little further over, hearing that funky tune I always liked, 'Lime in the Coconut.' "Jeez, heard it a thousand times though." I whispered, wishing I could just talk into the radio and tell the DJ to play something else. I dialed again in the other direction, not sure exactly what I was in the mood for, until I finally struck gold. It was the familiar guitar riff of, 'Smoke on the Water.' "Deep Purple, Yes! The Gods of Rock have answered." I said, wasting no time turning the volume all the way up, and raising my arms up towards the ceiling. Then I slapped my hands down against the desk and banged out the drum parts as hard as I could, singing, "Smooooke on the Waa-ter... The Fi-yar in the Sky-ee!" *Oh, to be a rock star,* I thought, banging the desk with my eyes closed and imagining myself standing on a stage in front of thousands of screaming fans...with long hair and tight leather pants, gripping the microphone to my mouth and belting out the lyrics while crazed girls reached out their arms towards me like I was a god!

"What's goin' on in there Bri?" came the voice of my mother from the other side of the bedroom door, bursting the bubble of my rock-star fantasy. "It doesn't sound like homework," she said, lightly tapping on the door with her fingernails, but not to Deep Purple.

Since my room was right next to the kitchen, it was near impossible to get anything past my Mom, but she was always cool about it. I got up from my chair and opened the door, and then sat back down as she stepped into the room and sat on my unmade twin bed. Turning down the radio I said, "Sorry Mom, I'm just trying to stay awake. Since seeing those drummers last night I just couldn't get to sleep, and now I'm tired and I can't think... I can't get this homework done!"

One thing I could always count on was that I could easily talk to my Mom about things and she would listen. According to my buddies, 'Mrs. McBride,' although she always insisted that they just call her 'Karen,' was considered very attractive for her age. "In the same way as Shirley Jones," Rob would tell me, "you know, the Mom in The Partridge Family." I didn't really think of my Mom in that way, but I guess I could see the comparison, since she did have the same short blond hair as Shirley Partridge and, although my Mom didn't really sing, she did have the same nice smile.

"You'll sleep better tonight honey," Mom said, "it's just great to hear that you're excited about something." I thought about telling her about my really weird dream from the night before, when I finally did get to sleep. I dreamt that I was marching in a parade with the LBJCB drummers, and I was trying to lift my arms to play the cadences, but they were really heavy, like I was under water or something. I just couldn't hit the drum on time, and the drummers were yelling, "Play it right, you're screwing it up!" As hard as I tried, I just couldn't control my arms. It was a real nightmare. I decided against telling her though, thinking it might be just too weird, even for my hip Mom.

"Yeah," I replied, "The same guy, Tom Masterson, is picking Rob and me up again on Thursday night and driving us to Millikan High School for the band practice. I'll get a drum and everything so I'll get to start marching and playing the cadences. I'm really excited about it...but I'm nervous about it too. I mean, these guys are really, really strong...they play so loud and it's not easy to get voted in. This one trainee, Mark, had to try out five times before he got voted in!"

My Mom nodded her head as she listened and then said in her usual supportive way, "Gosh Brian, you'll do fine...you love the drums and you're so good at it," she continued as she wiped her damp hands with the dish towel she had brought in with her. "Connie was telling me about the band and it sounds like a real good organization with a great bunch of kids around your age. I think it'll be a real positive thing for you." I figured it would be better not to mention the muscle cars, cigarettes, and massive dog pile on Mark McMullen. "I have to check on the dinner...we're having meat loaf tonight," she said and got up and stepped towards the door. "Do the best you can with the homework Bri and we'll eat in a few minutes. You'll sleep better tonight, I promise...and don't worry about Thursday night, you'll do fine. Just give it your best and have fun!"

*   *   *

Thursday finally rolled around and there I stood once again at the curb, anxiously waiting to be picked up at

5:15pm like we agreed so that I could meet Jeff before practice to learn cadences. I tried to ignore the pit in my stomach. *Going as a trainee sure is different than just going down to watch,* I thought, and tried imagining shapes in the clouds passing overhead to keep my mind off of my nerves. It had been raining all day up until just an hour ago, and I wondered if the band practice might be cancelled, but amazingly the rain stopped and the clouds broke apart revealing the first twinkle of stars. I wondered if Marvin Marker himself had some kind of arrangement with God. *You're funny, Bri,* I thought and smiled to myself as I zipped up my coat to keep warm from the chilly after-storm breeze.

Like clockwork at exactly a quarter after a vehicle screeched around the corner toward me just like a repeat of the other night, only this time it wasn't the white Mustang. It was a bright blue Datsun mini-truck, jacked-up in back with flared fenders and chrome rims, and three guys sitting in the seat up front. As it pulled up to the curb I immediately recognized Rob and Wally, but the driver wasn't Tom Masterson, it was his younger brother Sam, the bass drummer who played for Mark McMullen's tryout. Rob rolled down the window and said, "Hey Bri, Tom couldn't pick us up early after all, but Sam agreed to." Rob and Wally were sitting shoulder to shoulder next to Sam on the bench seat and I knew what this meant before Rob could even say anything.

"You mind riding in the back, Bri?" Rob said a little sheepishly, "I'll ride in back on the way home, promise.

Sorry bro." I looked at the truck bed and then over to Rob. The only things back there were a crowbar and a piece of rope. Sam turned his head toward me and then raised his left arm out the driver-side window, pointing to the back with a cigarette dangling between his fingers.

Oh well, beggars can't be choosers, I thought, and said, "Sure, no problem," and jumped up and over and into the truck-bed. I sat down low with my back against the cab, where the wind couldn't get to me as much. I was glad that I had my thickest coat on. I was also glad to be in driver training class at school and would be getting my license. This bumming a ride was already starting to get old.

Sam looked over his shoulder to make sure I was in position and then hit the gas and we took off for Millikan High School. Sam looked like a Masterson brother with short black hair and sideburns, and of course the brown and gold drummer sweatshirt, only he was much bigger than Tom and Wally. All I knew about him so far was that he was an awesome bass drummer and he was really cool for giving me a ride like this, even though I got the short end. I held on tight as Sam shifted gears and drove, the cigarette in his mouth creating puffs of smoke that whirled around to the back of the truck. The cigarette smoke actually smelled sweet from a distance. He had some loud music playing on the car radio and I didn't really recognize the song, but I think it was Frank Zappa.

Sam's truck was pretty bouncy as he drove through the dips and potholes of the streets of Lakewood. I had to hang on to the sides just to keep from sliding around. The custom front scoop scraped the street every time Sam hit a dip even though he tried slowing the truck way down to avoid that. Rob turned around to look at me every couple of minutes with a big grin on his face. *What a weasel!* I thought, knowing that he just loved this kind of stuff, watching me get jerked and bounced back-and-forth all the way to Millikan. I suspected that he was even telling Sam to speed up just to dick with me for a good laugh. Anyway, Rob turned around again and I shot him a look that let him know I would be getting even with him later. That just made him burst out laughing even harder.

Sam drove across town into Long Beach, headed down Spring Street and then turned right on Snowden Avenue. He hit the driveway dip of Millikan High School with one more scrape and pulled the truck into the parking lot with a final bounce of my butt off the metal truck-bed. He parked it next to the row of drummer cars, their warm engines still ticking as they cooled off under their sleek polished hoods. At least a dozen guys in brown sweatshirts stood leaning against the cars, talking and gesturing and laughing loudly. There were also a few pageantry girls with them, snuggled warmly under the arm of their drummer boyfriend, the gold pageantry sweatshirts pressed against the brown drummer sweatshirts. I wondered why they were here so early. *Must be just hanging out,* I thought as we bailed out of Sam's truck. Several sets of eyes turned in our direction and my stomach tightened. I felt real self-conscious all of a sudden.

"Hey Wubbie, what's up?" one guy asked, as he walked up to Rob and shook his hand.

I looked at Rob, puzzled. "Wubbie?" I whispered, "What's that?" Rob shrugged and said, "I don't know, I think I was telling one of the guys that I couldn't say my 'Rs' when I was a kid...you remember dude, I couldn't even say my name right, it was 'Wob' instead of 'Rob.' So anyway, one guy started calling me 'Wobbie' which somehow turned into 'Wubbie,' and it just stuck...it's been my drummer nickname ever since." That one blew my mind. Up until now any time someone at school made fun of Rob's speech impediment, he'd come out swinging punches at them. Now the drummers made a nickname out of it, and Rob was cool with it! I couldn't believe what I was hearing.

I recognized Lonny, Dave, Mark, and most of the other drummers right away, but some I still hadn't met. "This here's Brian McBride, tenor trainee." Rob announced to the group as we walked up to them. *Oh great, make me the focus of attention,* I thought, giving Rob another dirty look. I was nervous as hell and must have had the most bungled look on my face. I was face-to-face with the drummers and looking at their short-cropped hair, I suddenly felt like a total freak for having long blond hair down to my shoulders. Up close the drummers had an odd smell...it was cigarettes mixed with a variety of after-shave colognes, with an undercurrent of body odor. This was quickly becoming the familiar scent of 'drummer.'

"You already met Lonny, Dave and Mark," Rob continued, "this here is Ricky Spiegel, Ron Malave and his little bro Andy." Each guy gave me the drummer handshake as Rob said the name. "Greg Golson, Greg Pepoy… Karl Harkey and Joe Mehegan." They all looked at me, and I could tell they were sizing me up. The silence was excruciating. "Charlie Villegas, Gary Erbe…and last, but not least, your big bro Jeff O'Keefe who you've already met, of course."

I shook Jeff's hand last and blurted, "Hey."

He replied, "Hey what's up…good to see you made it early." One of the girls interrupted and said, "Hey what about us, Wubbie?"

Rob's face flushed and he said, "Oh, sorry… Bri, meet the gals, Evie Angel, Patty Berry, Sue Fowler and Cathy Castagna."

I figured the drummer handshake didn't apply here, so I just waved and said, "Howdy." like a dope.

All four just smiled and said, "Hiii Briiaan…" in unison. I felt my ears burning and knew my face must have turned twice as red as Rob's.

More silence, with everyone looking at me as if it was my turn to talk or something. *Oh please, someone say something,* I thought, and desperately looked towards Rob in hopes that he'd rescue me. Finally the tall blond guy Gary broke the silence by saying, "Well then, let's strap a drum on the chap and see what he can do." With that someone said, "here-here," in a British accent, another guy said, "Welcome to the section, TRAINEE!" and the others chuckled and went back to their conversations. Rob slapped a hand on my back and I felt a major load lift off my shoulders. It felt like I had just passed some kind of unspoken test. Something told me that this was just one of many, many more to come.

Jeff walked over to me and said, "Let's head over to the trucks and find a place to go over some cadences before practice starts. Here's an extra pair of sticks." He handed me an old pair of wooden snare sticks. Jeff had huge brown arms, a thick muscular neck, and a face that could either look mean or jolly depending on how he squinted. He walked light on his feet for his size, almost bouncing on his tiptoes like he could be a dancer or a football player or both if he damn well pleased. "We'll tap them out on the ground for now. Mind if I call you 'little bro?"

I nodded in agreement and said, "Sure." thinking with a smirk, *Who wouldn't you call little bro?...you're built like the fricking Incredible Hulk!*

I followed Jeff out of the parking lot and we walked along an open corridor between the school auditorium on the left and bungalow-style classrooms on our right. Up ahead I could see the two LBJCB band trucks parked right in the middle of an asphalt courtyard between two more buildings. One building had 'BAND ROOM' stenciled over its double-doors and the other read 'WOMANS

GYMNASIUM.' Even though practice didn't begin for forty-five minutes, band members were already pulling up in cars and heading towards the trucks.

As if Jeff had read my mind he said, "Sectionals…trumpet players, tubas, clarinets…the bandos, they also get here early to go over their parts before practice." Once again the dedication of these people blew my mind when you compared it to my high school band. *No wonder LBJCB sounds ten times better than Lakewood band,* I thought, *they're having sectionals while all we do in high school band is goof off before, during, and after band practice!*

Jeff and I walked up to the band trucks, which were a pair of older-model fifteen foot Ford moving vehicles, red & white with a huge 'LBJCB' logo painted on either side. An older gentleman opened the rear doors of both trucks, but there was no unloading of equipment yet. "Over here," Jeff said, and we walked over to a spot at the band room entrance. We sat cross-legged facing each other at the top of the concrete steps leading up to the band room doors. Jeff pulled a pair of snare sticks from his back pocket and twirled them with his big hands. *"TAPITY-TAP-TAP!"* He tested them on the concrete surface and then said, "I'll teach you rim beat first, then one-through-five, and if there's time you can learn Hendrix too, Okay?"

I nodded obediently.

"Here's the hand signal for rim beat." He stuck out his left fist with just the pinky finger pointing straight out. He then raised his sticks together in a cross and said, "On four, just listen this time," and with four clicks began tapping the beat on the concrete. I recognized the beat from the other night, though it sounded so much smaller when played on the ground instead of on drums. Rim beat was easy to learn, but then he started showing me one-through-five and that got tougher.

Jeff repeated one-through-five over and over, making me play it back to him until I got it right. Every time I screwed it up I'd say, "Shit, sorry," like a nervous tick.

He'd say, "Do it again," and we'd start all over.

As we tapped away on the concrete steps, bandos were walking past us heading towards the trucks. I finally got one-through-five down, so we worked on the cadence called Hendrix, and by almost six thirty I had learned a total of seven cadences. It felt pretty damn good, like Jeff and I were on a roll. "Seven down, twenty more to go," Jeff said, reminding me that we still had quite a ways to go. "We can go over the other cadences later, but you're learning pretty fast. Let's get to the truck and get you a drum."

We walked over to the trucks and this time there was plenty of activity. Band members were getting their instruments off of one of the trucks, while the drummers and pageantry girls were standing behind the other truck waiting for their drums and flags. There was an LBJCB staff member working each truck, hustling to get the equipment unloaded. They were the older men that looked like they could be the band member Dads. They were working up a good sweat reaching up to pull equipment off the shelves, then swinging their arms down to hand it to the person waiting below. From the trucks people were walking out towards the football field to line up at the running track for marching practice.

Each drummer yelled out his drum number one at a time, "Ten please," just like the other night at Vet's Stadium. While the guy in the truck pulled drum cases off of the shelves, the drummers were flinging their white drum straps over their shoulders. Like some kind of familiar routine the red sparkle drum would be handed down and the drummer would hook it to the strap and lower it to his knee in one fluid motion. With drum sticks or mallets in hand they headed towards the football field. For some reason I liked watching this organized action and noticed that the pageantry girls had a similar routine with their flags and leather flag harnesses. As they were handed the long metal flag poles with the colored flag wrapped tightly around it, they would twist the pole to unfurl the flag, letting it open up free like a sail in the wind before positioning it into the leather harness. There were pageantry girls walking with drummers, and it was fascinating to see the guys with their red drums and the girls with their tall flags, walking hand-in-hand towards the field like they were the 'kings and queens of LBJCB.'

Jeff and I stood in line, waiting our turn. Finally we got up to the rear bumper of the truck and Jeff said to the man who was wiping his face with a handkerchief, "Hey Jack, how's it hanging?" The guy nodded, then glanced at me briefly, and pointed an index finger to Jeff as if to tell him to grab a clue. "Oh sorry, seventeen please," Jeff finally said. "Hey Jack, this is Brian McBride, new tenor trainee. Brian, meet Mister Jack Bowen. Jack is Tom's Dad... Tom's a cymbal player."

Jack reached out a hard, callused hand and said, "Good meetin' ya Brian." We shook hands drummer style and he added, "I suppose you need a drum and some mallets, heh? Hang on, I'll see what I can find."

Jack was a stocky guy, muscular for his age with a moustache and dark hair trimmed in a crew-cut with a Brylcreem shine. He reminded me of a 1950's greaser. He wore dark blue pants with a short-sleeve mustard colored button-down shirt and black work boots. He clanged around inside the truck, looking through boxes, apparently trying to scrape up some drum equipment for me. "Not much drum equipment left," he shouted from deep inside the truck. "We've got almost thirty drummers now...including the trainee's... I've given away almost everything." After banging around some more, Jack finally came back carrying a tangle of objects in his hands. "Not much to look at," he said as he tried pulling the stuff apart, "but it'll work...hey, it's better than nothing, right?"

He handed me a pair of moldy leather work gloves, two bent mallets with frayed felt beater-balls, and a dirty old drum strap with a rusted clip. Then he disappeared into the truck and came back with the saddest, most beaten up looking red drum you could imagine. Its red sparkle finish was all scratched and faded, the chrome was dented and rusty, and the yellow chord was detached and hanging in a couple of places.

Jeff laughed out loud and slapped my back. "HA!" he said, "I guess it sucks to be a trainee, heh little bro?"

I looked the stuff over and shrugged, trying to think of something positive to say. "Well at least the drum head looks okay." I put the drum strap on, clipped on the drum, and adjusted the strap just like I had watched the other drummers do. Just having a drum...any red drum to bang on, felt bitchin' enough to me.

Overhead floodlights had clicked on over the football field, lighting up the track that surrounded it as a faded moon appeared to the East between tall Eucalyptus trees along a high chain-link fence. "Let's get out there, buddy," Jeff said, as he finished wrapping white first-aid tape around the last finger and then put on a pair of cloth under-liners, followed by a brand new pair of leather gloves, pulling each glove over his hand with his teeth.

We walked across the asphalt path towards the field and I followed Jeff and gazed with envy at his red drum glistening in the stadium floodlights. Compared to my jalopy of a drum shell, his was as shiny and beautiful as a brand new Ferrari with its polished chrome rims and shimmering red surface. *Some day I'll have that...a brand new red sparkle drum with all new equipment*, I thought, telling myself that these would be the trophies won for getting into this drum section.

I walked as fast as I could behind Jeff, and then we heard the drum major's whistle in the distance up ahead. "Let's go!" Jeff shouted, and lifted his drum and started running. I fumbled with the ratty gloves, mallets, and rusty bucket of a drum, trying to keep up with Jeff as seven drum cadences swirled furiously in my head.

CHAPTER 5

Jeff and I hightailed it to Millikan field and found the band lining up on the oval red-clay track surrounding the grass football field. Ranks of bandos stood between white chalk lanes meant for track runners. All of the equipment used for high school sporting events...pole-vaulting cushions, metal track hurdles stacked in a corner, soccer goalposts and even the empty grandstands, stood still in the shadows, the track now serving as an imaginary parade route. I figured that Marvin Marker must have gotten permission from the school Principal to use the track every Thursday night.

"Follow me," Jeff said, "I'll find a spot for you to march."

We walked to the very back where the drummers stood, and just as we reached the first line of snare drummers I tripped like an idiot over the concrete edge of the track. Barely catching myself and the drum hanging in front of me, I lunged forward in exaggerated steps, slamming my Adidas down so hard it caused puffs of red dust to fly out from under my feet. There was a gasp among the bandos and somewhere a girl screamed "Oh No!" but my arms flew instinctively in front of my face. In a split-second I recovered, grabbed the drum and stood upright. *As only a thousand wipeouts on a skateboard can teach,* I thought, and readjusted the drum back into place over my knee. "Good Save!" shouted one of the drummers as I limped forward.

"You okay, little bro?" Jeff said, giving me a concerned look. "Yeah, fine," I answered, even though my feet stung and I felt like the biggest dufus on the planet. *Getting off to a great start bonehead,* I thought as Jeff pointed to a spot for me to march behind him.

"Just follow me, watch for the hand signals and copy what I do," Jeff said and he took a spot directly in front of me in a rank of seven tenor drummers. Rob stood in front of Jeff in the snare line off to the left. Rob turned around and nodded at me, and I figured he must be jazzed to see me actually doing this, considering it almost didn't happen. For some reason I was sandwiched between two bass drummers and I hoped to the Lord of Mercy that those mallets wouldn't reach my face when they started throwing their arms out sideways, the way I had seen Sam Masterson wailing the other night. *I guess this is where the trainees start out,* I thought, noticing that the only rows behind me were the cymbal players, and behind them a row of pageantry girls with tall flags. Even though my nerves were in a bundle I was stoked to be standing here, and waited quietly for my first chance to hit the drum.

I watched as the last stragglers filled in the holes of the band formation. I expected to hear the whistle of the drum major at any second to step-off the band, but instead only heard the chaotic sounds of the bandos tuning their horns, and the hilarious banter of the drummers.

"Hey Spiegel," blurted Gary Erbe, the bass drummer to my right, "You're pants are drooping...what's the matter, can't you afford a belt?" The other bass drummers laughed like hyenas, tapping their mallets on the rim of their drums like it was their way of applauding. I stood frozen, hoping just to stay invisible. "Jeez," Gary continued, "Do I have to march back here and look at your dirty boxer shorts hanging out all night...is that supposed to motivate me or something?" More chuckles and bass drum mallets clacking. The target, Ricky Spiegel, stood in the snare line two rows up in front of Gary, and he was looking down at his pants and shaking his head. It was true, Rick's pants were hanging so far below his waist that his green boxer shorts were showing and the hemlines at his heels were all frayed from his constantly walking on them.

"Hey Erbe," snapped Rick as he turned around and placed a middle finger just under his left eye, "look into my eye," he said with a sarcastic grin, moving the finger up and down. "Bite me!" he said, and then attempted to lift his drum and pull up his pants as the other snare drummers watched him and snickered. "Go stand somewhere else if you don't like what you see," Rick said, and some guys turned to look back at Gary, waiting for his next snide remark.

"Why don't YOU move, Spiegel...better yet, come back here and march with the big boys!" said Gary, and I could see that Rick was rolling his eyes and just about done with this conversation.

"Dumb-ass bass drummer," he said, "Quick, throw him a slab of meat, he's getting hungry and restless." Rick then lifted his leg and ripped the biggest fart that I've ever heard. This made guys almost fall over laughing, and a couple of pageantry girls standing in back screamed, "Eeeeeuuww, gross!" Dave Geopforth, who was standing next to Rick, was leaning over his drum, laughing and slapping his leg. The cymbal players standing behind me were also cracking up as they practiced twirling their shiny cymbals high in the air.

"Hey, Ricky," Gary said, obviously steamed that the joke had turned on him. "I can outplay you any day of the week. How about we see who's still standing after this practice?" Rick's face turned from silly to serious as he realized the challenge...the gauntlet had been thrown down. "You're on Erbe." Rick replied, and pointed his snare stick at Gary like a sword. "Hope you can keep up bro...we'll see you in hell!"

"BAND, STAND AT...EASE!" The drum major finally yelled, and the joking and challenging stopped as every bando, pageantry girl, and drummer wiped the smile off their faces and brought their heads straight down. It became instantly quiet, except for the occasional squeak of a drum strap hinge whenever a drummer moved. I looked down also, checking through the corner of my eye to make sure my arms were in the right position. *Arms and mallets hanging to the sides, left beater-ball tip resting on the drum, right one resting on the hip.* I copied the others, and stood as still as possible, waiting for the next command. It seemed like the longest time before a voice broke the silence. It was Marvin Marker with his clipboard and megaphone, walking up to the drum major and mumbling his instructions. Finally the drum major spoke with a sharp, serious voice like an Army drill Sergeant. "Band, tonight we will march the track to get ready for the Knott's Berry Farm parade which is next week," he continued, "after that, we will break and meet in the band room to rehearse for the Shrine show, which is coming up in just five weeks. At that time, please turn in all band banquet money and your band council ballots. That is all."

Marvin cut in with his megaphone, now standing somewhere behind us. "Pazdernik, Oakley, stop talking." His amplified voice startled me. "Girls, what's with the giggling in the back?" I suddenly realized he was watching our every move while the drum major spoke. I could almost feel Marvin's eyes passing across the back of my head like a searchlight. I stood petrified, hoping not to be noticed.

"BAND!" the drum major barked, and raised his mace right up to his face. "A-TENN-HUT!"

"ROLL-BOOM! RAH!"

Everyone snapped their heads up and legs together so fast that I completely missed it. The drummers had crossed their sticks in front of their faces in the same instant, making a unified 'click' sound. A full second later came the 'click' from my sticks.

"Damn." I whispered, as a couple of heads turned in my direction. I missed the command. *What a dimwit.*

"Sloppy," the drum major scolded. "Get it right. Again, BAND...AT-EASE!"

Swoop! All heads were back down, all legs apart. *Won't miss it this time.*

"BAND...A-TEN-HUT!"

"ROLL-BOOM! RAH!"

Click! *Ah-hah, got it that time.* Heels together, head up, arms raised with mallets crossed directly in front of my nose. Everyone stood as still as statues. The only sound was the flapping of pageantry flags in the breeze.

"FORWARD, MARCH!"

Oh shit, here we go! Everyone lifted their left leg on cue, stepping forward to march. They became teen soldiers, ready to trample anyone who got in the way or walked too slowly, like me if I didn't get it together quickly! I missed the step-off completely and had to scramble my butt up to the line, or else get knocked in the head by a pair of flailing brass Zildjians as the cymbal players came up fast behind me. I felt like Gomer Pyle, trying to keep in step, but just blowing it, and waiting for Sergeant Carter to start chewing me out. The drummers went right into the clickity-click of the rim beat, but I missed the tenor part too. *Damn, too much all at once,* I thought, realizing how much easier it all looked when I was just watching from the sidelines. Marching with LBJCB was going to be a real challenge. It was much more precise and demanding than the high school band I was used to.

"Don't try so hard, just relax and go with it!" Charlie Villegas shouted at me from the bass line as he marched to my left, swinging his arms up and down gracefully as he played the rim beat. I struggled to get in step and find the groove, repeating to myself, "*Left, Left, Left-Right-Left...*" I watched Jeff up ahead just like he'd told me to. Copying his every move, I focused on playing the rim beat as I marched.

"Ba dum bum (chick) bum (chick) bum (chick) bum, ba dum bum (chick) bum (chick) bum (chick) bum..."

I closed my eyes for a second to just feel the rhythm and not try so hard, like Charlie suggested. I lifted my mallets and came down on the drum, playing the rim beat softly just as I had memorized only a half-hour ago. At first walking in step while playing the new cadence was as difficult as tapping your head while rubbing your stomach, but I stayed with it until I finally just *listened* and got the coordination down. I opened my eyes to find that I was marching in step and playing the beat at the same time, without even thinking. *I'm doing it!* I thought, and was thrilled to feel the flow of my legs marching in step with everyone else, and the swing of the drum up and down on my knee while bringing my mallets down just right. The drummers were sounding off the majestic approach of LBJCB and I was now a part of it!

What a rush! It was way up there man...like the day I learned how to ride a two-wheeler bicycle back when I was seven years old. Same feeling of freedom...my Dad and I walking my blue Schwinn Stingray over to Hoover Jr. High one Saturday afternoon with my dog Brando trotting behind us, and Dad finally takes the training wheels off the bike and says, "Today's the day, son." and balances me up on the white banana seat. I start pedaling while Dad runs behind me holding the sissy bar, but the more I think...the more I *try* to balance the bike while steering and pedaling, the more I just tip over and have to start all over. Dad finally yells as he's pushing, "Just keep pedaling son, look straight ahead to where you want to go and don't think about anything else!" So I stop thinking about all of the separate parts and just point the bike like he says, and all of a sudden the bike balances effortlessly under my legs. I pedaled the full length of the schoolyard before realizing that Dad had already let go. By the time I looked over my shoulder he was waving at me a hundred yards back, the dog barking wildly next to him.

"Much better!" Charlie shouted, noticing that I had pulled it together and was finally marching in step. LBJCB made a full circle around the track, the drummers playing the rim beat while the band members focused on keeping their ranks straight and swinging their arms up and down. Some twirled their brass instruments round and round in the air just for show. Then Lonny kicked it up a notch and held up a hand signal. It was one-through-five, the set that Jeff had just taught me. It was as if Lonny knew exactly what cadences I had learned earlier and went straight for them. *No time to think about it, here we go!* The rim beat ended and I braced myself for the three-count that would lead into the next cadence. I raised my arms to the sky and prayed that the mallets would hit the drum on time.

"RAT TATTA TAT-TAT-TAT, BAM TATTA TATTA…"

I was surrounded by the violent force of full-throttle percussion. The sound swallowed me up and the adrenaline rush was incredible! It was like being trapped in the middle of a hurricane, as twenty-six drummers dug into their drums all at once. The snare and tenor drummers flailed wildly in front of me, as the cymbal players crashed loudly from behind and the bass drummers swung their mallets dangerously close to my face on either side. My eardrums were screaming, but I ignored it and marched straight ahead, trying to bring my arms down as hard as I could. *Don't try so hard, just feel it,* I repeated to myself, and swung my arms in unison with Jeff. I wanted desperately to get it right, to play the drum cadences with them without screwing it up. For the first time I was inside the syncopated machine of the LBJCB drummers, and it was unreal…the most powerful feeling that I had ever known. I didn't even know why these guys hit their drums so hard, or why I was so attracted to it, but I just wanted to hit the drum as hard as I fricking could! Maybe it was something I needed to get off my chest…the frustration I felt at school...my poor grades and the people that made me feel like a total outcast. Maybe every drummer had some personal reason for hitting his drum with all of his might...something that just pissed him off and that needed to be taken out on the skin of his red sparkle drum. All I know is that these guys were dead serious about it and every fiber of my body wanted to offer a piece of myself to the cadence, and be a part of this strange tribe that took their violent rage and turned it into such an incredible sound.

We marched on. I played one-through-five as loud as my scrawny body would let me, pounding on the trainee drum while hoping that my legs would do their own thing to keep in step. My mallets were slamming all over the drumhead at first, but I worked to aim at the center and dug in for all it was worth. As the final beats of the cadence approached my muscles started to really burn and I felt the first sting of new blisters on my hands. I looked out to the other tenor drummers and they were playing louder than hell, like they were just getting warmed up and could go on forever! *How can I possibly keep up with them?* I thought with real fear. It was just like the nightmare I had the other night...my arms were suddenly so heavy, and there was so much further still to go.

I pushed myself to finish the last cadence of the set the best I could, but my arms just wouldn't lift any higher. I let out a frustrated grunt at the end of the cadence. Just as I was trying to fathom playing another cadence, the drum major mercifully threw out a hand signal and the drummers brought their arms down for the 'Roll-off' drum beat that transitioned into a song. The band swung their instruments up in unison and started blasting out the theme from 'Patton' with their horns. *Whew!* I thought, bringing my arms down and trying to shake the burn out of my muscles. *And that's only one set of cadences. Shit!* I watched the tenor drummers twirl their mallets up in the air like helicopters, coming down on the drum just in time for the on-beats of the song. *Wow, mallet twirls…no rest for the arms?* I thought, and watched the snare and bass drummers also doing fancy flips and twirls with their sticks. They could be delicate with their sticks as well as forceful and I had to admit that the twirls looked cool. I tried to imitate the twirling with my tenor mallets, but they just kept tangling up and smacking me in the head. There was so much going on that it made my head spin. I still doubted that I could live up to this level of drum playing, yet wanted Lonny to keep throwing more at me. I had to prove myself with these guys, and I just hoped there would be enough time to learn all this stuff before my first tryout.

After playing 'Patton,' which was a bitchin' song, we went right into another set of cadences and I was back inside the hurricane. I didn't know these cadences yet, so just worked on marching in step with my arms crossed, and watched the drummers pounding their brains out. I noticed Marvin watching from the bleachers, standing with several other staff members and occasionally speaking into the megaphone. "Straighten those lines, guide up!" he'd say, "stand up straight when you march...and tighten your butts, like you're holding in diarrhea!" *Now there's a pretty thought,* I winced.

"Come on you wussies, Wail!!" Sam Masterson yelled from the far right side of the bass drummers while he cranked away on his drum.

"We'll see you in hell Masterson... Yeee-oooww!" Greg Pepoy yelled out in response, and I'll be damned if those tenor drummers didn't throw their arms up higher, with Sammy riding them like that. One tenor drummer even broke his drumhead, and everyone screamed, "Yeee-haaahh, all right Golson!" and the guy raised up his gloved fists like a boxer, a big grin across his sweaty, flushed face. I realized that breaking drumheads was actually a *goal* with these guys.

We must have circled the track at least three more times before stopping, although I was so tired by then that I had stopped counting. The drum major alternated his commands the whole way, from a song into a cadence, and then a cadence back into a song again. Finally the drum major blew the 'step-in-place' whistle command, "TWEEEEEET-TWEET!" and every person stopped abruptly on the soft clay dust, still marching in place. The drummers also continued marching in place, while still pounding out the last half of the cadence. I missed the command completely and took two clumsy steps forward, almost smashing into Jeff's backside with my drum before

I figured it out and stopped. *Tap the head while rubbing the belly,* I kept repeating in my head, frustrated by my embarrassing lack of coordination. The drum major turned to face the band and marched in place, then lifting his mace overhead with both arms, he blew the 'halt' whistle command, "TWEEEET-TWEEEET-TWEEEET!" and the drummers responded with another roll-off cadence, "Roll-Boom-Roll-BOOM-BOOM!" bringing the band to a complete stop.

Silence...other than drummers catching their breath and flags flapping. Sweat dripped from my forehead, quickly turning cold against my skin in the chilly night air. The blisters on my hands stung and my legs trembled...my right shoulder hurt from the weight of the drum strap, but I stood as still as I could, just like everyone else. Then I heard the click of Marvin's megaphone and his voice pierced the air, "Okay I want musicians to get to the band room as quickly as possible. Take five for a bathroom break if you need to." He flipped through pages on his clipboard. "Pageantry girls, meet Mrs. Bullock in the mirror room to go through the dance numbers for the Shrine show. Concert drummers, I need you to rehearse with us tonight. Any new drummers who can sight-read percussion parts on sheet music, meet in the band room also. And the rest of you drummers..." The megaphone clicked off and I could tell Marvin was weighing something in his head. *Yeah, like maybe what to do with a bunch of restless drummers to keep them from loitering outside the band room,* I thought with amusement. Another click, indicating he'd made up his mind. "Drummers, you may use the choir room for a drum sectional, but keep the doors closed! I don't want the noise coming into the band room."

"Frick yeah, choir room practice tonight, boys." Someone whispered excitedly, and the drummers looked energized again. Rob slapped a low-five with the guy next to him.

Marvin lifted the megaphone again. "Okay Mister Pyka," he said to the drum major, "whenever you're ready." There was another long pause, and I was hoping that we'd be dismissed soon because I really had to go pee. "BAND, DIS-MISSED!" *Thank you Lord Jesus.* "STEP-TURN-BOOM!" yelled the whole band, and the tight marching formation dissolved away into nothingness again as people headed back to the band room. The drummers stayed put though, awaiting a command from Lonny. The drum section had their own thing going, and I thought it was fascinating that they were allowed to be a group within a group and do things completely separate from the rest of the band.

"Drummers," Lonny spoke with his sticks still crossed at his face and his head turned to the left, "when I dismiss you I want the concert guys... Malave, Geopforth, Golson, Erbe, to meet me at the trucks to unload the timpani drums and all the other crap." Another pause, as Lonny figured out what to say next. "I want the rest of you to get in the choir room ASAP and learn Dave's new cadence, Lefty. If you get it down good enough tonight, we'll march right into the band room and play it for Marvin and everyone...blow 'em all away!" *Cool, this one I get to learn with the rest of them,* I thought, glad that I'd get a chance to watch how they actually learned a drum cadence as a group. "DRUMMERS...DISMISSED!" Lonny shouted, and we step-turn-boomed and headed back through the narrow gate of the stadium towards the band room. Some of the pageantry girls stayed behind just to walk back with their drummer boyfriends, rolling up their flags while they chattered away. I lagged off to the side to let them pass, keeping my eye out for a bathroom or even just a good bush to ditch behind. Jeff saw me and hung back to join me. "How'd it go little bro?" he asked as he wiped the sweat off his face with his sleeve.

"Not bad. Think I'm starting to get the hang of it." I replied, feeling fairly confident in my answer. "Good," he said, "get ready for some more. We'll get in a circle and bang our brains out for a while, work on endurance...then learn Dave's cadence. It's supposed to be a real ass-kicker." I wasn't going to tell Jeff or anyone how wiped out I already was.

"Great." I said, thinking this was no time to be a wimp. If they were going all the way, I was going all the way too, even if they had to scrape me off the floor.

Jeff walked up ahead of me to join the other tenor drummers. Rob appeared a moment later, holding hands with a cute sandy brown-haired girl with hazel eyes and a fair complexion. My eye caught a glance from the dark-haired girl walking next to her and my heart jumped. She was beautiful.

"Hey Bri, this is my girlfriend Dena Wellman," Rob said proudly. Dena smiled at me with a twinkle and a snap of her chewing gum.

"Hi Bri," she said, and then turned to the slender figure walking next to her, whose brown eyes were so pretty that I couldn't take mine off of them, "this is my friend Laura Villegas…she's Charlie's sister," Dena said, "Laura, meet Rob's best friend Brian McBride."

I was speechless and my face felt like it was burning. I awkwardly lifted a gloved hand and waved a mallet in the air like a robot. "Hi Laura," I said, hoping that I didn't look too thrashed and sweaty from playing drums, like some wet dog just out of the rain.

"Hi Brian," Laura said, "I saw you marching tonight, sorry you almost fell." She ran a hand through her thick black hair and I noticed her pretty slender fingers and the pink polish on her nails. "I march in the back row behind the cymbal players," she said, "You were doing great. You're gonna be a great tenor drummer!"

I must have blushed ten shades of red. *She's so pretty, and she thinks I'm gonna be great.* I tried looking into her eyes, but like a reflex the shyness took over, and I looked downward, then to the left at Rob's smirking face, and then nervously back to Laura as Dena's gum kept snapping noisily. There was a warmth and kindness in those eyes though...beautiful almond shaped brown eyes, with such a sparkle. "Hey, what can I say," Laura said with adorable wit, tapping her flagpole on the ground as she talked, "I just know talent when I see it...yep, I sure do." Suddenly I realized that there was no reason to feel nervous, not with this girl, and the tension I usually felt around girls just relaxed like magic.

"Thanks," I said, "I have a long way to go, but I'm gonna do my best." I realized that with Laura taking notice I was even more motivated, and nothing in hell was going to stop me from getting into this drum section now.

"You'll do great," Laura said warmly, "I predict no more than two tryouts, max. Nice to meet 'ya Brian...see you later, maybe after practice?"

I replied, "Sure," and nodded more than I needed to. As she walked with Dena towards the band room I took another glance at her silky black shoulder length hair and exotic brown skin. I could see the resemblance to her brother Charlie, but beyond that there was no comparison...she was stunning...a total fox! I memorized the lines of her smile...her full lips and pretty teeth that reminded me of Cher the way they sparkled when she smiled. I outlined every curve of her tall, trim dancer's body with my eyes. *The kind that fills in a pair of mint green Dittos perfectly,* I thought, and my stomach started to burn all of a sudden.

"You can peel your eyes off her now," Rob said, pushing my shoulder and snickering like he always did.

"Shut up, turkey," I replied, feeling actually more proud than irritated this time. I continued watching Laura and the other pageantry girls head towards the mirror room. Just as Laura reached the door, she turned around, looked straight at me, and with a broad smile waved at me before disappearing inside.

"Wow... Charlie's sister," I sighed under my breath, waving back to no one at the mirror room doors. I had completely forgotten that I needed to pee and lost track of just exactly what to do next.

Dena let out a little giggle and Rob came up to me and whispered, "Yeah, and she just split up with a trumpet player too...guy named Robert." He raised his eyebrows up and down like Groucho Marx. "Pretty cool, heh?" he said, then pulled on my sleeve and pointed towards the building. "Come on, let's get over to the choir room," he said, and as I followed Rob, Dena jumped onto his back for an instant piggy-back ride. He grabbed a leg on each side, and started trudging forward, drum on and all.

"What did you tell him Robert?" Dena pleaded, "Come-onnnn, tell me!" Rob just shrugged and tightened his lips together, as Dena started pounding on his back, almost making him lose his balance. We walked past the band trucks with drums in hand, and Dena jumped off and headed for the mirror room as Rob and I joined the drummers who were filing into the choir room.

"I think Laura digs you, man," Rob said, and slapped my back as we walked up to the choir room doors. "You're one lucky trainee that's for dang sure."

I looked at Rob, and then down at my drum, not quite ready to believe what he was saying. So much was happening all at once that I couldn't decide which was more exciting, being a drummer trainee or meeting Laura. I could barely keep myself from jumping up and down like a happy freak-azoid. I thought of the cartoon dog that flies up into the air every time he gets a biscuit. Then I realized that I still hadn't gone pee.

"Chee-yaa, right Rob," I finally replied, "So where the hell is a bathroom around here?"

Rob pointed towards the building marked 'MENS GYMNASIUM' and I ran as fast as I could with my drum still strapped on and banging painfully against my leg. I reminded myself that I was just a peon trainee, and to just cool it with these Laura thoughts for now. *First-things-first,* I thought, knowing that I needed to focus... I had tryouts to think about, and no use even thinking about getting closer to Laura Villegas until I got voted in as a drummer.

Still, my mind hung on to the chance of seeing her after practice...just to look at her face again and hear her soft voice...and I hoped to God that I would think of something interesting to say if I did.

CHAPTER 6

I ran down the long hallway to the gym bathrooms, kicked open the men's-room door and then unhooked my drum and set it down. Pulling off my mallets and gloves, I stuffed them in my back pocket and then leaned over the nearest stall to finally relieve myself. "Whew!" I exhaled, realizing at the same time that I was dying of thirst. I quickly washed my hands at the sink and tried to ignore the sharp sting of the grainy pink powdered soap on my blistered hands. "Ouch, damn that smarts!" I said, and looked at my own weary image in the mirror. *You've got a long way to go, Bucko,* I thought, as I slapped water on my face and hair. I leaned over the sink and took several large gulps of cool water which tasted metallic, but was better than nothing. Grabbing a wad of paper towels to dry myself off with one hand, I picked up my drum with the other and quickly walked out across the deserted school quad toward the light of the band room.

There was a hustle-bustle of drummers working to unload equipment from one of the trucks using a ramp that had been lowered in front of the band room doors. "Watch-it, watch-it, don't let it roll down too fast!" Dave was yelling, as he and Gary slowly rolled a top-heavy copper timpani drum down the ramp, trying to keep it from tipping on its tiny wheels. The outside floodlights cast beams of light onto half a dozen drummers standing ready to muscle a bulky equipment box marked 'Percussion Instruments' down the ramp with Jack Bowen helping. I noticed Marvin standing next to a red Ford Country Squire station wagon. It had laminated wood side paneling and an 'LBJCB' decal on the front bumper and I figured that it must be his car. Several LBJCB staff members stood around Marvin, sipping coffee from styro-foam cups, chuckling and talking in adult voices that were somehow comforting...like hearing your own parent's voices in the kitchen at night as you're falling asleep, their presence assuring you that things are alright.

I walked up to the well-lit band room and looked in, my eyes squinting from the brightness of the overhead fluorescent lights. I saw that most of the bandos were already inside, taking their seats and arranging their music stands in an 'orchestral' half-circle around the conductor's podium. Ron Malave had already assembled a drum set and was playing an incredible drum solo at half-volume with his eyes closed, head cocked sideways and a self-assured grin across his face. *Multi-talented drummer.* I thought, as I watched in total amazement. The choir room was just a few feet away from where I stood, connected by a concrete walkway and metal overhang. I could see why Marvin told us to shut the doors before drumming. The sound would shoot straight into the band room like a sonic boom.

"Let's go drummers!" Lonny shouted from the choir room doors. I entered the room and immediately noticed how stuffy the air was. The room had no windows, only a narrow row of vents along the ceiling that were closed, making it feel like a sauna. One of the guys was trying to reach a latch that would open a vent, but it was too high. It was dark in there too, like a dungeon compared to the well-lit band room. I wondered why Lonny had only flipped on a single row of lights. *Dark drummers,* I thought with some amusement. The walls and ceiling were covered with grey acoustical panels, and there were rows of chairs rising up just like an old movie theater on the left. On the right the drummers were pushing aside music stands, a portable chalkboard, and a grand piano on rollers across the black linoleum floor to make room for the drum circle. I chuckled to myself, thinking that the choir director probably didn't have a clue about the abuse his classroom took after-hours...the assault of the drummers pushing their way in and bouncing their high-decibel noise off the delicate fiber panels that were designed for singing voices!

I clipped the red sparkle drum back on, and then took the smelly damp gloves from my back pocket and pulled them over my raw hands. I cussed at the sting of the blisters, reminding myself to get a new pair of gloves before the next practice, since the old rags Jack had given me were just crap.

"Over here," Jeff said, gesturing me to stand next to him in the circle, "and I'll get you some masking tape for those gloves." I walked over and took my place facing the center of the forming circle. Jeff handed me the roll of tape, and I wrapped each glove several times to cover the holes, and then strung a tenor mallet snuggly around each glove. Crossing my arms to my chest, I waited quietly as the others took their places.

More damp brown sweatshirts and body odor, as the last guys entered the humid room. The only missing drummers were the six guys in the band room rehearsing on timpani, concert snare and other assorted percussion instruments. I wondered if Dave and the others liked being in there, listening to Marvin say, "Take it from the top!" all night while we got to crank out more cadences in the choir room.

The circle of drums took up the entire space of the choir room with nothing in the middle except the scuffed linoleum floor, the stagnant air, and my silent attention. The tenors were standing to my left, cymbal players to the right, and the snare and bass drummers arched all the way across the room to complete the circle. When Lonny saw that everyone was inside he kicked the door shut, slamming it loudly with a "KA-CHUNK!" that made me flinch. It was like he was saying, "No one goes out…and no one comes in." He took his place with the other snares, and any last murmuring stopped as the drummers shushed each other into complete silence.

"DRUMMERS…READY!"

"Click!"

The drummers snapped to attention and all eyes focused toward the center of the circle. Mallets crossed at my face, I held my breath against the intense silence in the room, as the energy shifted to a seriousness that I can only describe as some kind of ceremony. The stuffy, half-lit choir room now seemed more like a tribal 'sweat lodge,' the kind that I had read about in National Geographic, that the Indians built for their meditation rituals.

"Drummers," Lonny said, breaking my deep thoughts. "We'll play cadences until we're good and tired, work on endurance," *Like we aren't already exhausted from marching, Lonny,* I thought, looking straight ahead, anticipating the oncoming pain, "and I want you all to concentrate on the tempo, since that's what goes first. The fatigue sets in on the final stretch of the parade route and things start to drag down like a funeral march." I waited for the hammer to fall, for Lonny to call out every cadence that I had learned over and over, bringing me to the embarrassing moment of truth when both arms would finally give out. "One through five, on my count." he commanded, and I heard the four clicks of the drumsticks that would begin another brutal session. I tried to ignore the image in my head, of me collapsing on the floor in front of the drummers and being forever dubbed the 'biggest pussy trainee of all time.'

Lonny clicked off the four-count and someone flatly said, "Here we go," and we went right into the rumbling cadence. As the volume cranked up I immediately realized that every beat of the drums was amplified at least ten times inside the choir room. The loud part of the cadence kicked in and I was surrounded by flailing arms and a wall of sound, the floor shuddering under my feet. I watched as music stands danced across the room from the vibrations as we pounded and pounded on the drums. It was so insanely loud in there that I just laughed inside as my ear drums throbbed, and I just closed my eyes and surrendered to it. Swinging my arms up high in the air and trying to ignore my sore hands, I hit the pocketed surface of my red drum as hard as I possibly could.

Standing inside the firestorm of sound created by the drum circle, I took in the strange altered state of actually *feeling* the concussion of cadences bouncing off every inch of every surface of the stifling hot choir room...violent explosive sound trapped like canned thunder. It was like being down in the bowels of a battleship, the insane booming and churning of the engines and boilers...the sweaty, grease-covered men laboring over the heat and the fire. I looked out at the strained faces of the drummers, guys with sweat streaming down their faces screaming at each other, "Come on God-dammit...is that all you've got?!" as they thrashed and grunted and hammered away at their drums. I noticed Mark McMullen playing with his eyes closed and his teeth clenched. His brand new drummer sweatshirt was damp with sweat and his whole body looked soaked to the bone. We were only a few minutes into it, but every part of my body was too tired to go on...my hands burned and the heat and the stink of the room was so suffocating that my head was spinning as my lungs gasped desperately for air. One guy, a snare trainee that I hadn't met yet, actually stopped and sat down. His face was as white as a sheet and someone yelled, "Get up trainee!" but he just sat there trying to catch his breath. I figured his days were numbered if he didn't get up and get back into the drum circle immediately. I was hanging on by a thin thread myself, but somehow the shouts of the drummers kept me going. There was something contagious and almost addicting to the act of pushing yourself to the limits, proving yourself on drums. I just had to keep up with these guys, and I knew that they were watching... I knew that I must keep trying!

We went from one cadence to another in a vicious drum marathon that seemed to go on forever...past any point of reason. *Just...hang...on...* I said to myself as we played Hendrix, and looked over at Jeff and Rob who were also straining to keep their arms up, trying just to hang on. I glanced over at Lonny, hoping for a sign that he might end this craziness, but saw nothing but a face of stone and two black marbles for eyes...he was merciless. He threw out another hand signal and I thought I might puke at any second. Luckily it was a cadence that I hadn't learned yet so I stood at attention looking straight ahead. Even though I was taking more breaks than the others, the heat and the noise and the physical exhaustion was taking its toll. My brain was delirious from the fatigue and I thought desperately, *This is crazy. Why am I doing this? I don't even have to be here!*

Just as I was ready to drop face first to the floor, crying like a little girl, Lonny swiped a drumstick across his neck, indicating 'drummers stop.' It was the most beautiful thing I had ever seen in my life. The last beat of the cadence finished with more grunts and groans, and every guy brought their legs together and stood at attention as the noise vibrated into silence. Although I was shaking and fighting to keep my forearms raised and sticks crossed at my face, I was just glad to still be standing. *I made it!* I thought, taking in deep breathes and trying to recover. I noticed that the trainee who had sat down was gone and wondered if he had just given up and gone home. The room was silent except for the huffing and puffing of drummers and the humming in my ears. I looked up at the wall clock and couldn't believe that less than an hour had passed.

It was like being in another dimension, standing inside of that choir room. *Tribal sweat lodge,* I thought again, realizing that choir room practice was no doubt another important drummer ritual. Even though I was in survival mode as a trainee, just trying to learn cadences and keep from fainting, I was starting to realize that there was more to syncopated drums than just playing loud. The drum circle was like a ceremony, only instead of eating peyote and chanting like the Indians I had read about, the drummer ceremony was this extreme test of physical endurance...a marathon of playing cadences and challenging each other to the point of total exhaustion. This reached a fevered pitch until the heat and suffering and primal rhythms all came together in a spiritual release…with every drummer offering up his energy to the total energy of the room. As a trainee witnessing this I was completcly amazed. Although the challenge of playing syncopated drums totally intimidated me, almost leveling me to my knees, I was grateful to be a part of the drummer ceremony…to join in the strange ways of their private inner-world.

"Drummers…at EASE!" Lonny shouted, and the drummers dropped their arms to their sides like rag dolls. "Take five, and then meet back here to go over Lefty." he said, and all I could think of was getting out of this hell-hole and finding a cool drink of water. "Drummers, POST!" Lonny said, and with that guys started unhooking their drums and setting them down carefully on the floor at their feet, propping them up by the leg rests and keeping the circle formation unbroken. Lonny flung open the choir room doors and I could hear the muffled musical sounds of the band rehearsing across the way. It sounded like they were playing the theme from 'A Chorus Line.' I ripped off my mallets and wet gloves, set my drum down, and threw everything inside the shell of the drum. Guys were wiping their faces with their sweatshirt sleeves as they silently headed for the door, too tired to say anything.

"Killer session, eh little bro?" Jeff whispered through his heavy breathing, as he shook out his wet hair and combed his hands through it. I could see flushed cheeks even through his dark skin.

"I'll say," I gasped, bending over my drum with my hands on my knees.

"Come on, let's get some fresh air," Jeff said, and I followed him toward the doors. As we stepped out of the choir room, a heavenly blast of cold air hit my face and it gave me new life.

"Aaaaaaahhhh..." I said, looking up at the clearing night sky and flapping the bottom of my t-shirt up and down to let in some cool air. Although I still felt dizzy and weak, breathing in the fresh night air made me feel so much better that I knew that I would recuperate. I was just damn glad that I had not fainted in front of the drummers. I had survived another round.

We were all dying of thirst. I followed Jeff over to an ancient porcelain drinking fountain attached to the stucco wall just outside of the band room. The other drummers were already huddled around it, waiting for their turn to take a much needed drink.

"This piece of crap fountain has no water pressure, but it's all we got unless you want to go find one somewhere else?" Jeff said.

I had better luck with the mens-room sink, I thought, but just as I was about to suggest this to Jeff, Lonny shouted, "Hurry up drummers, another couple of minutes then let's get back inside!" *Damn, better stay put,* I thought, and stood patiently with Jeff while guys took turns stooping over the spigots to get to their tiny trickles of water.

"Com'on man, save some for us!" someone shouted as Gary and Charlie took their turns. The guys standing in line were goofing off and started push fighting, not realizing that they were almost falling on top of Gary and Charlie.

"Back the frick off!" Gary yelled irritably and he and Charlie started shoving guys back.

As they finished getting their gulp of water, someone said, "Sorry man," and things settled back down, but for a second there I thought that someone was going to lose a tooth on a spigot and start a drummer fist fight.

I was the last in line, but finally got my turn. I leaned over the fountain for as long as I could, letting the slow trickle of water flow into my mouth while resting my head on the cool porcelain surface. Then I stood up and stretched out my back, wiped my face with my shirt sleeve, and then headed back towards the choir room.

"Let's get back in there," Jeff said as I walked up to him, "this won't be as wicked as that last session though...not at all." he said, and I was relieved to hear that.

I smelled cigarette smoke and looked around to see where it was coming from. I saw Sam Masterson and Greg Pepoy just around the corner from the choir room, sneaking a quick smoke and talking intensely about something. I couldn't imagine smoking a cigarette after a drum marathon like that.

"That smoking stuff will kill ya," Jeff said, noticing the delinquent smokers too. "Hope Marvin doesn't catch 'em. He'll send them home if he does." Jeff's attention turned towards me and I could tell that he wanted to say something, but wasn't sure how to say it. "Now don't freak out or anything little bro," Jeff continued, "but I just talked to Lonny and he wants you to tryout at this Sunday's practice."

I could feel the color draining from my face. "What!" I blurted, and a couple of the drummers turned their heads towards me. I lowered my voice and leaned towards Jeff, trying to hide my panic. "Why so soon? I mean, isn't that too..."

Jeff interrupted by putting his hand up to my face. "Hey dude, relax...it's no problem...that's actually a compliment. Lonny wouldn't suggest it if he didn't think you could learn most of the cadences by Sunday." Jeff glanced to the left and the right, and then whispered, "Besides, no one gets in on their first tryout, so it's good to get it out of the way. You seem to be picking it up fast, so we just need to work overtime in the next couple of days to teach you the rest of the cadences. Especially with the Shrine show coming up dude...you just need to go for it!"

Holy crap! I thought. I really, really wanted to be a drummer, but a tryout this Sunday? Jeff made it sound so easy, but inside my gut was churning. I figured that I had no choice... I had better just go for it, otherwise it would look like I was a big wuss. "Well okay I guess, if you say so," I replied, hoping I didn't sound too scared.

"Hey man, don't worry about it," he said with a slap on my back. "Just trust me. I won't let you make a jack-ass of yourself in front of the guys. It makes me look bad too, you know." Realizing that his hand was now wet from slapping my sweaty shirt, Jeff wiped his hand on his pants, saying "Gross dude!" with a disgusted expression. "Anyway, don't worry, I'll teach you every cadence between now and Sunday." We stepped back into the choir room with the rest of the drummers and clipped on our drums. "Practice is at Vet's stadium," he continued, "one o'clock instead of six thirty. Let's get there an hour early and we'll go over everything one more time before your tryout."

Even though things were moving a lot faster than I expected, I felt relieved knowing that Jeff was willing to work with me like that. We stood waiting for Lonny, as the rest of the guys put their drums back on and grabbed their sticks. Jeff turned and whispered to me, "Lonny's bringing Dave in, since Dave wrote Lefty and so he's the best guy to teach us. We'll get it down before we go into the band room and play it for Marvin and the bandos. That's how we've always introduced a new cadence in the past." I looked at Jeff's hulk-like body and chuckled to myself, thinking we must look just like George and Lennie in *Of Mice and Men* standing next to each other. I hoped that I had made the right move by choosing tenor drum.

Dave Geopforth entered the room carrying his snare drum. The other five 'percussionists' filtered in behind him, clipping on their drums and taking their places in the circle. Lonny entered last and shut the doors. "Christ it stinks in here," Dave said, waving his hand in front of his face. "The Right Guard is failing you, boys."

Someone mumbled an insult about pansy concert percussionists and there was a wave of chuckles, but Dave just ignored it. He clipped on his drum and stepped out into the middle of the circle. Dave did look too fresh, clean and dry compared to the soggy, sweaty drummers. It was almost like he was above this choir room stuff...like maybe he'd rather write the cadences, and then have us kill ourselves playing them. He took a pair of wooden 2-B snare sticks from his back pocket and tapped on his drum, "TAT-TAT!" as if to get our attention, and then he looked out to the drummers and cleared his throat.

"Now listen up ladies. I'll play the whole cadence for you like we did before, then we'll all try playing it softly." Someone in the bass drum line sneered at the part about playing the cadence softly and Dave shot a glare in that direction. "I guess we're gonna be dickheads tonight, aren't we?" he snapped, staring at the bass drummers, but not knowing for sure who made the comment. He then turned his attention back to what he was trying to say. "Now pay attention, here's the hand signal." He stuck out his middle finger like he was flipping someone the bird. Everyone laughed at that, and Dave raised his hand even higher in the air. "I don't want any of you jokers forgetting the hand signal, so I picked a familiar one," he said, and I tried to imagine how Marvin would react to Dave's hand signal, or the people watching along the parade route. "I've named the cadence Lefty. It's from a Maynard Ferguson tune called Left Bank Express. Now listen, here's how it goes..."

I was amazed to hear that Dave got the idea for a drum cadence from a jazz song, and wondered if this was how all cadences started out. Dave tapped Lefty out softly on his drum and we all watched and listened, some guys swinging their arms in the air to imitate him. Then he had the snares repeat their part, and then the tenors, followed by the basses. Finally he showed the cymbal players when to come in with their crashes, and then we played it together from the beginning until it was sounding pretty damn good.

Lonny glanced up at the wall clock, noticing that it was almost nine o'clock. "Guys, practice is almost over." he said, then looked over at Dave. "Marvin will want to know if we're ready?"

Dave looked out across the circle and saw heads nodding enthusiastically. "Yes we're ready," he said, "we just need to try it once at full volume...tell Marvin two minutes." Lonny disappeared with a slam of the door, and all eyes were on Dave. "Let's try it full throttle before going in there," Dave said. "Ready? On my count." With four sharp cracks of his snare sticks to set the tempo, the bass drummers slammed down hard on the first beat with a startling roar.

"BOOM-BOOM-BA-BOOM-CRASH...BOOM... BOOM-BOOM-BA-BOOM-CRASH... TATTA-TATTA!!"

The cymbal players crashed right on cue, followed by the snares laying down their machine-gun sixteenths as the tenors answered with their rhythmic gun-shots...and it all came together like a symphony of detonating explosives! I had chills up my spine as I played it, and knew right then that Dave was a great cadence writer, concert-percussionist or not! The cadence came to a peak and then ended in a wild flurry of snares, tenors and bass drums all flailing in unison. The moment of silence that followed was electric, as everyone stood there speechless...grinning and catching their breath.

Sam finally broke the silence by saying, "That's a damn bitchin' cadence Dave!" and everyone else let out loud hoots in agreement as Dave just stood there beaming.

"I think its ready boys, nice work," Dave said, looking satisfied as his alert eyes scanned the circle. "You got one more in you?" he asked, and everyone shouted excitedly, "Frick yes!" in response. Dave brought his legs together and his sticks up. "Good, then just follow me. We'll march single file into the band room, spread out along the back wall, and then show them how it's done!"

"Drummers, READY!"

"Click!"

"Rim click... Forward, MARCH!" Dave shouted, and the drummers began moving forward in half steps, hooting and hollering, "That's right, kick some drummer ass tonight!" The excitement in the air was intense with anticipation, as we marched out of the choir room and towards the band room, ready to play Lefty for the first time to an audience. With each step of the left foot the snare drummers clicked their sticks on the chrome rims of their drums, as we headed single file towards the band room. Like clockwork Lonny appeared, swinging open the double doors of the band room and wedging them in place before strapping on his drum and taking a spot behind Dave. Lonny let Dave lead the drum section into the band room, no doubt because it was Dave's cadence. I also figured from what Rob had told me, that Lonny was getting the guys used to the idea of Dave being the next head drummer. Dave had a way of getting the drummers psyched-up using just the right words at just the right time. There was no doubt in my mind that we would all follow him anywhere he asked us to go.

Dave marched into the band room, half-turned left, and carefully stepped up the three flat tiers on the left side, making his way towards the back wall with the rest of us following. The band room was also stuffy from having about a hundred human bodies in it, but it wasn't half as bad as the choir room. The fluorescent lighting overhead made everything seem unreal and the room had a strange odor…kind of musty and sour. I wondered what that smell was, until I noticed the bandos sitting there with their musical instruments, the spit dripping from the valves onto the floor. *Gross!* I thought, and glanced down at the green carpeting, trying not to gag.

Marvin stood front and center at the conductor's podium, flipping through sheet music as Dave led us along the back wall and across the whole length of the band room. The bandos fidgeted in their chairs, some putting away instruments while others watched and whispered as we clicked in behind them. Dave marched to the other end of the room and then stopped. Still marching in place, he made a sharp right pivot facing the center of the room, and each drummer behind him did the same like a domino effect all the way to the last cymbal player on the other side. "Drummers, HALT!" Dave barked, and every drummer stopped in place with a final click and then it was silent.

Marvin finally looked up and around the room, seeming quite proud of the size of his marching band. Two clarinet players were murmuring under their breath and he glared at them until they stopped. Then a band room door squeaked opened and a pageantry girl peeked her head in. I could hear the whole pageantry corps talking and giggling just behind the doors. Marvin's eyebrows raised and he slowly turned toward the doors.

"Yes...may I help you dear?" Marvin said sarcastically, making some of the bandos giggle and the pageantry girl turn bright red with embarrassment.

"Sorry we're late," she said sheepishly. "We lost track of time."

"Ah, well...so nice of you to join us Miss Crosley," he continued with a mischievous grin, his thin white conductor's baton tapping in his hands. "Would you girls like a formal invitation, or are you going to come in now?"

More bandos chuckled as Marvin rolled his eyes and turned to face the band with a playful wink. The doors swung open and about fifty pageantry girls filed in one after the other...gold sweatshirts, tan legs, and red sneakers tip-toeing behind Marvin to the far corner near where Dave was standing. They dropped to the floor one-by-one, sitting Indian-style as if they were at a slumber party. I watched each girl enter, then spotted Laura and my heart raced. I took in every detail of her beauty as she gracefully moved across the room and sat with the other girls. Her face was slightly flushed from dance practice and it made her look even prettier. Suddenly I couldn't wait to wail on my drum playing Lefty. I would smash my mallets down on that drum as hard as I could so that Laura would notice, no matter how much it killed my body!

The doors slammed shut behind the last pageantry girl, and then the drum major stepped in front of the entry way like a guard standing watch. Marvin looked down at his clipboard, glanced at the clock on the wall, and then back to the bandos. "The drummers have a new cadence to play for us, and then I have just a few announcements before you go home." Ignoring the groans from the bandos, he looked over to Dave. "Whenever you're ready, Mr. Geopforth," he said, and from the corner of my eye I watched Dave lift his sticks to count off Lefty.

The first beat sent a shuddering boom through the band room that made the bandos jump in their seats. I threw my arms into it and ignored the pain. Every drummer around me strained to thrash out Lefty as everyone watched and listened, many covering their ears. Lefty sounded loud and dangerous and perfect, and Dave grinned through his gritting teeth in his moment of victory. Even Marvin seemed impressed as he stood there smiling, his arms crossed and his head slightly nodding as he listened, not able to hide his own pride over his awesome syncopated drum section.

Playing Lefty used up my last ounce of energy and I realized that it had been one hell of a drum practice, but that I had survived. With my first tryout coming up I knew the time had come for me to get serious. *Time to learn the cadences, get a haircut, and be a LBJCB drummer!* I chanted to myself as I swung my arms.

Looking out over the heads of the bandos, my eyes met Laura's. I realized that she was watching me, and she was smiling. Unable to smile back, I put every last bit of remaining energy into the final beats of Lefty, and stared deeply into her sparkling brown eyes as the explosion of drums caused white flakes of acoustical ceiling to float down on us like snow.

Brian & Rob Pre-Drummer Days 1970

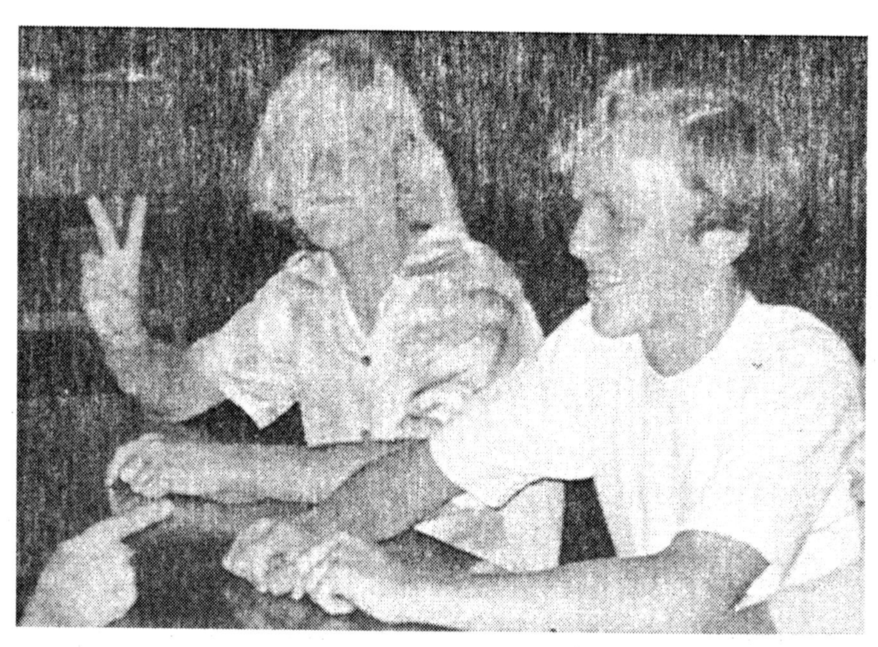

Trainee Brian & Drummer Rob 1976

Long Beach Junior Concert Band 1976

Drummers & Pageantry Girls 1976

CHAPTER 7

The ceremony called 'drummer tryouts' was about to begin on a breezy Sunday afternoon at Vet's Stadium on the 8th of February. Practice had ended at 3:45pm and there was a scurry of band members putting instruments away, staff members loading up the trucks, and cars heading out of the parking lot. The sun hung just over the Douglas airplane hangars to the west and the breeze was getting colder by the minute as the drummers huddled in front of the trainee. There stood the nervous trainee with a red sparkle tenor drum hanging from his shoulder, arms crossed with gloves and mallets...and twenty sets of eyes leveled at him. The bass, snare, and cymbal player stood patiently behind him in tryout formation, while Lonny stood front and center facing the trainee, twirling his stick. The tension was so thick that I felt bad for the trainee. In fact, I was downright terrified for him, because this time the trainee was me!!

The scene was just like McMullen's tryout had been the previous Sunday, with the drummers staying behind until the rest of the band packed it up to go home. Jeff had walked me across the stadium parking lot to a concrete path that ran along the back side of Long Beach City

College, which was adjacent to Vet's Stadium. Huge oak trees lined the path, dividing it from the grass soccer field that had served as the prime location for McMullen's initiation. "Right here's good," Jeff said, pointing to a shady spot under one of the oak trees. The tree had a crooked trunk that jutted out almost horizontally before rising upward. It didn't fit in with the perfectly upright stalks of the trees on either side. *Misfit tree,* I thought, and wondered if this was a bad sign.

Arms crossed with new gloves and hair trimmed short, I nervously waited for my first tryout to begin. My body already ached from marching practice and there was a double layer of tape covering blisters on both hands, so I knew that this was going to be a new lesson in pain. Jeff had told me that a cymbal player, Ron Malave's younger brother Andrew, was also supposed to tryout on snare drum, but he didn't make practice for some reason so it was just me today. Some guys were still putting their drums away so I waited with a pit in my stomach the size of a football and cadence hand signals flashing in my head. This seemed to be how the drummers liked to start each tryout, by making the trainee stand there scared shitless, getting totally psyched-out. Glancing up at the blue sky I took a deep breath, prayed, and tried to relax while retracing the events of the past couple of days.

*　　*　　*

Since I had to learn the cadences fast over a two-day period, Jeff and I needed to spend as much time as possible going over everything before my first tryout. I had just gotten my driver's license, so Jeff came up with the brilliant idea that I be his 'trainee chauffeur,' that is, drive him wherever he needed to go in exchange for his teaching me the drum cadences. Even though I didn't have much driving experience yet, I agreed to do it because it seemed like the only way I was going be half ready for my tryout on Sunday. My Dad had actually let me borrow his older model 1962 diesel Mercedes '190-D,' a white four-door with grey leather interior and a chrome front grill, the familiar Mercedes emblem fixed proudly on the hood. It had been my Grandfather's pride and joy until he died in '64. When my Dad inherited the car it became the 'extra' vehicle sitting in the driveway and since it was still in pretty good shape, I got to take it out once in a while. It was actually the perfect car for learning how to drive, especially with its manual transmission. I slowly learned how to work the clutch and the 'four-on-the-tree' stick shift, which for me was a real trick at first. The car was a trip to start up too, with its solenoid coil in the dashboard that burned bright red before you could yank the pull-starter to turn over the engine. The car was a real dog off the line...not quite up to drummer 'muscle car' standards, but it was as solid as a tank. I guess my parents figured I couldn't get into too much trouble with such a sluggish automobile.

Anyway, now that I was at Jeff's mercy, I started driving him to school, which meant getting him all the way to

Millikan High and then back-tracking it three miles to Lakewood High in hopes of getting to my first class on time. At around 7:30 am on Friday morning I pulled up to Jeff's house, honking the funky sounding German horn of the car. Grasping the steering wheel, I noticed how tired and sore my arm muscles felt from the drum marathon in the choir room the night before. Jeff came out of his front door with a slam of the screen and took a long look at the faded white 190-D four-door idling at the curb, it's diesel motor clacking away and smoke billowing out of the tail-pipe into the chilly morning air. He giggled as he opened the door and jumped into the passenger seat, saying with a grin, "Hey what do you know, it's Mr. Magoo…or shall we say, Mc-Goo!"

I shook my head at his wise-ass remark as I tried pulling the steering column shifter back up into first gear. "Yeah go ahead and make a joke," I replied, "but would you rather ride bikes and freeze your butt off on a morning like this?" He pushed on my arm and said, "No way little bro…no complaints dude, none whatsoever. I'm just messing with your mind. This is the lap of luxury man, for sure. It's a fricking Mercedes!" He tilted the seat back a couple of inches and said in a very bad German accent as he waved his arm up, "Onward Herr Kommandant…to Millikan, the great school of stoners!" Finding first gear with a nerve-racking grinding sound, I slowly let out the clutch pedal and the car lurched forward. With a puff of black diesel smoke in the rearview mirror I drove the

'McGoo mobile' while Jeff yacked my ear off about the mechanics of playing tenor drum.

I continued down Carson Street, turning left on Studebaker and then heading out to Spring Street towards Millikan High School. I was sweating bullets all the way, trying not to pop the clutch and stall the car at the intersections. While I drove Jeff drilled me on cadence hand signals and we also tapped out the cadences, me pounding on the steering wheel while Jeff banged them out on the dashboard. I pulled up to the curb at the front of Millikan High and we noticed some of the students staring at us and making snide comments about the McGoo mobile.

"Losers," Jeff said as he opened the car door, "if anyone tries to mess with us I'll pinch their heads." This stuff would have bothered me before, but for some reason I didn't give a damn what people thought now. I had bigger things on my mind and what these jerks didn't know was that I was going to be a LBJCB drummer and they had better not screw with me. Jeff stepped out and straightened the collar of his striped OP shirt, saying, "Thanks for the lift bro...see you right here, same place, twelve o'clock for lunch. We'll go over more cadences." I gave him a thumbs-up and turned the car around, thinking, *Sure glad he's on my side,* as I made my way through the morning school traffic and back towards Lakewood High School.

I parked on Harvey Way near Lakewood High since the school parking lot was already full. Checking my watch, I realized that I had less than one minute to get to class. "Damn!" I said, and quickly grabbed my books, locked and shut the car door, then ran towards the building where my Semantics class was about to start. Running across wet grass and past the other hurrying students, I made it up to the English building and reached for the door handle as one of the campus 'narcs' rolled by on his cruiser bicycle. He waved at me and said, "Hurry it up young man, the bell's about to go off...we don't want to see you gettin' written up for being tardy, heh?" I waved and flew open the door, hauling past the classrooms on either side as the 8 am bell went off.

At the other end of the hallway I spotted Rob, who was also rushing to get to class on time. He had the English composition class right next door to mine. He wore his drummer sweatshirt as always, which made him easy to spot. "Hey Rob," I said, slowing to a walk and trying to catch my breath, "I thought you'd beat me to class for sure since I had to drop off Jeff."

He stopped sharp at the classroom door and put his hand on the knob, saying, "Would have, but my damn ride fell through... Mark was supposed to pick me up but his alarm didn't go off. I've never pedaled my bike so fast in all my life!"

He was referring to his buddy Mark Bergendahl, who actually lived right up the street from me. Rob had introduced me to him a couple of years ago and the three of us had gone to summer camp together, but I hadn't seen much of Mark since then. Rob was leaning heavily on Mark lately, trying to recruit him into the drum section. I hadn't seen Mark at band practice yet, but thought it would be totally cool if all three of us were in the drum section together.

"Anyway," Rob continued, "maybe I can bum some rides from you next week, since you now have wheels."

"For sure dude, no problem," I replied, adjusting the textbooks that were slipping from under my arm, "as long as you don't mind me dropping off Jeff first?"

Rob nodded and then asked, "Hey, how's it going with Jeff anyway?"

"So far, so good," I replied, "we worked on cadences this morning and we're meeting for lunch and then again after school."

"Cool Bri, if you need any help just let me know," Rob said, lowering his voice to a whisper, "I know the snare parts and can help you to learn any cadence, any time."

"Thanks man," I said, "maybe I'll take you up on that, depending on how it goes with Jeff."

"Just say the word, it's no problem." he said, and then pushed open the classroom door. "Oh by the way Bri," he said with a smirk, "beat ya' to class... I win, you're the loser ha-ha!" He disappeared behind the door and I scoffed before stepping into class two minutes late.

As agreed, I picked Jeff up for lunch at twelve and we cruised through the nearby Jack-in-the-Box on Spring Street for burgers, fries and Cokes. We parked it and stuffed our faces while watching the girls walk by, and then tapped out more cadences on the dashboard. The dashboard already had cracks in it, but Jeff's pounding was causing the outer vinyl layer to chip away, exposing the yellow foam underneath. I hoped that I would learn the cadences before it got too thrashed.

I had already learned rim beat, one-through-five, Hendrix-swing and of course Lefty, so we focused on Linda, foot, Candy, Lucy and step-off-number two. Jeff then showed me roll cadence, new cadence and Sandy. I was finding that each cadence was unique and featured a different drum. Candy and Lefty were bass drum cadences that shook the ground like a sonic boom, while foot and Sandy showcased the machine gun snares. Of course my favorites were tenor cadences like Hendrix, new cadence, and Linda…they hit you like a punch to the chest. They were the ultimate call of the warpath on the street.

After school I chauffeured Jeff around town and we even made the rounds visiting some pageantry girls that Jeff wanted me to meet. One girl was named Patty Berry. I think Jeff had the hots for her because he was laying it on pretty thick. The other gal was named Carol Crosley and she was real friendly and cute, but all I could think about was finding where Laura Villegas lived. Laura and I had talked after band practice on Thursday night, and I was kicking myself for not getting her phone number. *Next band practice, you fool,* I promised to myself.

The next morning I picked up Jeff bright and early, and we spent most of the day repeating the same routine…driving around in the McGoo mobile while Jeff quizzed me on the hand signals, then pounding out the cadences on the steering wheel and dashboard before driving through J-in-the-B for munchies. By the time I had learned all of the cadences, the dashboard of the Mercedes was beaten down to the metal frame where Jeff had been hitting it with his drum sticks. There were pieces of foam everywhere and I knew that I would be paying for it, but just hoped that my Dad and my dear old Grandpa in Heaven would understand. I knew that my Dad wouldn't like the looks of it, but would tell him that it was the only way I was going to be able to learn the cadences from Jeff in such little time. Jeff and I agreed that the old 190-D needed new paint and upholstery anyway, so we figured that thrashing the dashboard was a small price to pay for the opportunity to learn the LBJCB cadences and to be ready for my first tryout.

*   *   *

"This is Brian McBride's first tryout on tenor," Lonny said, his deep voice snapping me out of my daydream and bringing my focus back to the stark realization that the drummers had surrounded me. "I want everyone to keep it quiet and pay attention," Lonny said, and I took a slow, deep breath through my nose and tried to ignore the twenty sets of eyes that stared back at me.

No turning back. I thought, as Jeff stood off to my right

whispering, "Remember what we went over little bro...relax and concentrate, and you'll do fine!"

Rob was standing off to my left, and he gave me a thumbs-up and then lifted his arms high up in the air, indicating to me, "Keep your arms up...up!" I noticed Dave and Sam standing behind Lonny, whispering something back and forth. Mark McMullen stood by himself near Rob with his arms crossed, probably very relieved that this was all behind him. Everyone had cleared out except for Jack Bowen standing next to the LBJCB equipment truck across the way, and the drummers waiting to witness my pain. Charlie Villegas, Ricky Spiegel and Wally Masterson had volunteered to play for my tryout, and they stood behind me in complete silence. The sun had disappeared behind the Douglas hangars and the air was cool, which was a good thing considering that the heat was definitely your enemy during a tryout.

I stood there feeling as self-conscious as a mouse in a cage, sure that I had jumped into this too soon. *How did Jeff talk me into trying out this soon?* I thought, in a sudden panic, and realized that my legs were trembling. I ignored it and looked straight ahead with no expression, trying to hide my fear...trying to copy exactly what I had seen McMullen doing during his tryout.

When everyone was quiet Lonny looked straight at me and threw the first cadence hand signal. His thumb pointed straight up and his forefinger pointed at me like a gun. My mind blanked out at first and panic rushed over my body, but somewhere in my jumbled head it finally came to me. *New Cadence!* I thought, and somehow managed to come down on the drum just in time, answering the fourth click of Lonny's stick. My tryout was underway. Some of the drummers were sitting on the concrete sidewalk watching, others stood smoking cigarettes, and a couple of guys paced back and forth looking downward, listening more than watching...but they were all studying my every move. I stared out at the mass of brown sweatshirts and, parting my legs for good balance, dug in with the mallets and prayed that my arms and my memory would hold up.

Lonny called one-through-five next and then Linda, while the drummers shouted, "Come on...is that all you got?! Don't puss out now trainee... PLAY!!" I tried to look straight ahead and not get distracted and screw things up, but my mind blanked out right in the middle of one-through-five and I had to stop completely. I managed to jump back in at the start of number four and finish the set, but then totally forgot how to play the first part of Linda. *Damn it!* I thought, as I desperately tried to save face and jump back into Linda. With everyone looking at me the pressure was just too much and my mind blanked out again. I froze, not remembering a single beat of Linda. *How could you forget Linda? It's a tenor cadence!* I thought, as Jeff shouted, "Come on man, don't stop... Linda, you remember LINDA!" Luckily I remembered it half way through and jumped back in and recovered. Lonny shook his head and threw his fist up, calling Linda again, obviously wanting to drill it into my thick skull. I played it again as hard as I could out of sheer frustration, my arms now burning with fatigue, yet hoping that this would somehow make up for my screwing it up like that.

Lonny was doing his best to break me and it was working...my arms were getting heavier and I felt like a wind-up toy monkey whose spring was slowly uncoiling until the tin drum was barely being tapped. He threw more hand signals... Hendrix-swing, Sandy, then Candy, and then more rim-beat into step-off-number-two...and although the cadences were coming to me now, I couldn't lift my arms past my nose. Sweat was stinging my eyes and new blisters announced themselves painfully on my hands, but I knew that I couldn't just stop...the drummers demanded my best effort even if I got too tired or forgot a cadence.

"Come on, get 'em up!" yelled Greg and Karl, and although I kept swinging my arms up, I couldn't grip the mallets anymore. They came down feebly all over the drum head, making the drum wobble out of control on my leg. My forearms and biceps were so completely numb that I had to use my upper shoulder muscles just to keep my arms swinging upward, while lifting my body by the tip-toes in a desperate attempt to fight gravity. *I'm so thirsty,* I kept thinking, my throat feeling like sandpaper. I pictured a tall glass of ice water, but that only added to my torture and so I struggled to push it out of my mind. I couldn't even imagine playing drums like this in a thick band uniform down a long parade route on a hot summer day. It was just like the choir room experience the other night...feeling like I could drop flat to the ground at any second. I was back in that same fatigue-induced delirium, only this time there was nothing mystical about it...no spiritual 'high points,' only desperation. I actually hated syncopated drums in that moment, thinking, *Why does it have to be so fricking hard...why are you putting yourself through this...couldn't you have just stayed there on the sidelines watching the drummers...now you have to go trying to BE a syncopated drummer...are you fricking crazy?!*

The drum was defeating me. I was so exhausted that a part of me wanted to just give up and go running home to cry under my pillow. Something else inside of me just couldn't accept not getting into the drum section...so I hung on. I grunted and strained and continued to make a complete fool of myself in front of the drummers, hoping that they would at least see just how badly this weakling misfit trainee wanted in. Finally Lonny showed mercy and ended the tryout with a swipe of his drumstick across the neck. I played the last beats of step-off-number-two and then brought my legs together and mallets up, barely able to cross them at my face. My clothes were wringing wet, I was shaking with fatigue, and my chest heaved in and out uncontrollably as I gasped for air. *Tenor drum takes too much out of you,* I thought, feeling totally trounced, *too much torture...you're not strong enough to be a tenor drummer...you should have listened to Lonny.*

The three guys standing behind me, Charlie, Ricky and Wally, were also breathing hard after playing straight through all of my flubs without stopping. Charlie said through his heavy breaths, "Good effort, McBride, nice try," but his encouragement barely registered in my foggy mind.

There was some murmuring of drummer voices as they all waited for Lonny. Finally Lonny said, "Okay Brian, good effort. Go ahead and sack your drum and wait by the truck while we vote." Lonny then barked, "Drummers...DIS-MISSED!" and the four of us yelled, "Step-Turn-BOOM!" I let my arms and head drop down as the drummers followed Lonny up the sidewalk to a spot under another oak tree, to vote on my clumsy attempt at playing the tenor drum.

I walked across the street over to the band truck and handed my drum up to Jack Bowen, who was waiting patiently for the drummer tryout ritual to end. Jack glanced down at me from inside the rear of the truck as he put the drum back in its case, and said, "Hang in there buddy...you didn't do too bad for your first tryout. I've seen much worse."

I nodded and replied, "Thanks, better luck next time I guess." Hearing Jack's words gave me hope, but I knew in my heart that I had blown it. *Forgetting Linda of all things!* I thought, shaking my head in disgust. I knew that Jeff would ride my butt about that one...messing up a tenor cadence. I just couldn't believe the difference between banging cadences in the car and playing drums for a real tryout in front of the drummers. It was like night and day. The only good news was that I hadn't passed out, which was one of my biggest fears. I told myself right then and there, that as long as I was still standing after Lonny threw everything he could at me, then I could at least say that I had survived.

The drummers huddled under the oak tree for what seemed like only a couple of minutes, and then they split off and started walking back towards the parking lot where I was waiting near the band truck. I knew that the decision had been made and my gut churned again. Even though I didn't expect to pass on my first tryout, there was still a feeling of disappointment that I just couldn't shake.

Jeff and Rob walked up to me as the other drummers headed for their cars. Jeff shook my hand and said, "Well buddy, you didn't make it in tonight...but hey, we knew that, right?" I nodded as I heard the actual words, and let it sink in. I began wondering just how many tryouts it was going to take to get voted in.

"Look at it this way, "Jeff continued, "at least your first tryout is behind you." Rob chimed in, "He's right Bri, it's done. You broke the ice. Besides, no one gets in on their first tryout anymore...only two guys that I know of ever did, Sam Masterson and Joey Mehegan...but those days are long gone. The next one will be easier Bri, trust me on that one." Jeff flashed a sly grin and said, "Right, and next time you won't forget LINDA!" He flicked the top of my head with his paw-like hand and the three of us chuckled. "Tryouts are pretty freaky, aren't they little bro? It totally messes with your mind!" Jeff said, and I realized that he had been in this situation before too. Having Rob and Jeff there meant a lot, and their encouragement helped to ease my incredible self-doubt.

"We're also gonna be doing some strength training bro," Jeff continued, "push-ups and chin-ups...build some muscle on those skinny arms of yours. You need more staying power dude." *He's right.* I thought, and nodded in agreement. After the choir room experience and now with my tryout, I knew that I had a long way to go in the stamina department. With hulks like Jeff, Karl and Greg in the tenor line, I had to get serious about building up my strength or else they would just bury me, especially during parades. I mean, those guys were strong...it seemed like they could play cadences forever!

"We'll talk tomorrow on the way to school," Jeff said, "Lonny wants you to tryout again, but not until after we march in the Knott's Berry Farm gig next week. That gives us more time, which is good. By the way, you going to that?" I didn't know anything about a Knott's Berry Farm performance, and realized that I needed to get my hands on an LBJCB schedule right away.

"Sorry bro," Rob interrupted, "I should have told you about it, but it's a parade we're marching right down the middle of Knott's. We'll be marching all the way through the park and end up at this brand new ride called the Parachute Sky Jump, where we'll perform for the opening ceremony. Trainees are welcome to come to the performances any time…not to play of course, but to ride on the bus and watch the gig and all."

It sounded pretty interesting to me, a chance to actually check out a uniformed LBJCB performance and see Laura again. "Sure, when is it?" I asked, and Rob replied, "Next Saturday at noon. The band meets at the Arbys restaurant parking lot on Spring Street near Millikan at ten o'clock, where the buses will pick us up. You should go dude…we can drive over together, and I'll even get you a seat on the drummer bus!"

I was totally relieved to find out that I would have a few extra days to get ready for my second tryout. I knew that I had a long way to go, and the more time I could get with Jeff, the better. Feeling totally spent and ready to go home and drink a gallon of water, I walked towards the McGoo mobile as a cold breeze hit my wet clothes, giving me a chill. The drummer muscle cars were firing up all around me like angry monsters and began pulling out of the parking lot, each one screeching and burning rubber as they headed out towards Clark Avenue. One guy tapped out part of a drum cadence with his car horn, sounding out the snare intro to one-through-five, "Beep-Be-Be-Beep-Beep-Beeeep!" as he gunned it down the street. Rob and Jeff were waving at Jack as he pulled the bulky LBJCB equipment truck out of the stadium parking lot, its rear wheels bouncing dramatically over the edge of the curb.

"Ready little bro?" Jeff said as he ran up to the passenger door of the car.

"Yep, let's go," I said, and dug for the keys in my damp pants pocket.

Rob ran up and yelled, "Hey Bri, can I bum a ride home with ya, if my bike will fit in the trunk?" I came around to the back of the Mercedes and opened the trunk and looked inside. The trunk was huge…it looked like two bikes could fit in there easily.

"Sure, no problem," I said and helped him lift the bike into the trunk, angling the front wheel so that the trunk lid would close. Rob yelled, "Shotgun!" but it was too late… Jeff had already claimed the front passenger seat. Rob jumped into the back as I yanked on the solenoid starter knob to fire up the diesel motor.

As I pulled out of the Vet's Stadium lot, Jeff and Rob were chatting away about pageantry girls while my weary mind wandered. As painful and exhausting as it was playing syncopated drums and going through these tryouts, it was also the most gratifying thing that I had ever done in my life…and something inside of me was becoming more obsessed with it. There was nothing even close to this drum section or LBJCB, not at school, not at the YMCA, not anywhere. To become a syncopated drummer was a major accomplishment and I knew that it would take everything I had to get in, but the more that the tenor drum tested me…the more blisters, sweat, and pain that it caused…the more strangely possessed I felt by it. I didn't expect people to understand this…hell, I wasn't sure that I even understood it.

CHAPTER 8

The days after my tryout were a hectic daily schedule of eating, sleeping and living for drums. Jeff drilled the cadences into me, over and over until they became like second nature. I got to the point where I was playing cadences in my dreams. He also made me do strength training like he said he would. We'd drive the McGoo mobile over to Hartwell Park after school, and I would do four sets of push-ups on the grass, followed by four sets of chin-ups on the monkey-bars. "Come on little bro, give me three more reps!" Jeff would yell, as he leaned his bulky figure against the swing-set sipping his large Coke. He also made me run laps around the park until I could barely walk back to the car. Even though Jeff's trainee 'boot-camp' was leaving me wiped out every day, I could feel my body slowly gaining strength in the arms and lungs, and I sure as hell wasn't having any trouble getting to sleep at night. I knew that I was going to be just as anxious standing before the drummers a second time, but this time I would also be that much more prepared.

The next band practice was on Thursday night at Millikan field for marching rehearsal, since the Knott's

Berry Farm parade was coming up on Saturday. Jeff moved me up from the bass drum rank and planted me right in the tenor rank between himself and Greg Pepoy. LBJCB must have marched around that track a dozen times that night, playing every song they knew, and when the drummers got their chance to play cadences, Jeff and Greg rode my ass hard. "Come on trainee, get those arms up!" Greg would yell as we kicked up red clay dust and wailed. Lonny called out Hendrix, Linda, and all of the others while Jeff made sure that I had the correct sticking and stayed in step.

Playing cadences while marching created more fatigue in the hips and legs than just standing and playing because you had to use the lower body to control the tenor drum. This made it a double-dose of stress and strain. I used muscles that I didn't think I even had, and after practice I told Jeff, "Man, just when I think I've been through the most brutal drum playing session there could possibly be, the next practice just kicks my butt even more!"

Jeff just chuckled and slapped my back, saying, "Stand-by little bro…wait 'til we add on the uniform and shako in the hot sun, with the asphalt melting your feet all the way down a three mile parade route…then we'll talk about brutal drummer hell!"

*   *   *

My second tryout was set for Sunday February 22nd at Vet's Stadium practice, the week after the Knott's parade.

I was so focused on that day that I could hardly concentrate on anything else. At least I had the Knott's gig coming up on Saturday which I looked forward to watching even though I couldn't play drums. I was bummed when I didn't see Laura Villegas at Thursday's practice and found out from Dena Wellman that she was sick with the flu or something. Laura was supposedly feeling better and was going to try to make the Knott's performance. I hoped to get the chance to talk to her then.

But the biggest shocker of the week came on the Friday after Millikan practice. Rob and I were at school walking to the cafeteria to get lunch, when he asked, "Hey Bri, you wanna come with me to a drummer party tonight?" My jaw dropped to the ground when he said that, because Jeff had told me that drummer parties were totally off-limits to anyone but the drummers...and that included girlfriends, bandos, cymbal players and especially trainees!

"Hell yeah Rob, but I thought trainees weren't allowed?" I said, and began wondering if he was trying to set me up for some kind of trainee hazing.

"Yes that's true," he replied, "but I told them that you would stay out of the way and keep quiet...serve them a couple of beers now and then, help to clean up, and they said yes. Come-on man, it'll be fun!"

There were some strings attached just as I had suspected, but I didn't question it any further. I figured that if Rob had worked out a way to get me into a drummer party, it was just another golden opportunity to see what went on inside the drummer inner-sanctum. Recovering from my initial shock, I replied, "Well then okay, count me in!"

"Great, can you pick me up tonight at around six o'clock since Jeff can't make it?" Rob said with a grin, and I realized with amusement his other reason for inviting me. This chauffer trainee thing was becoming a real tradition. "Sure, no problem Rob," I said, shaking my head and wondering how I was going to convince my Mom to loan me her station wagon for a few hours, since the Mercedes was in the shop getting a tune-up.

After school I told my Mom about the drummer party and asked to borrow her car, and surprisingly she said, "Sure, I don't need the car tonight. Just be home by eleven, okay?"

I jumped up and down and gave my Mom a hug, saying, "Thanks Mom! Yes I'll be home by eleven sharp, promise!"

*   *   *

That evening at about 4:30 pm I slowly backed the yellow 1968 Oldsmobile Vista Cruiser wagon out of the driveway and headed down Carson Street towards Cherry Cove to pick up Rob. Unlike the diesel Mercedes, this car had a 350 V-8 under the hood along with power steering and brakes, so I had to adjust accordingly since it was ten times more touchy. Pulling up to the curb of Rob's house, I saw that he was already standing at the front porch waiting. He had a way of always making me feel that I was running late.

"Right on Bri!" Rob blurted as he opened the door and hopped into the passenger seat. "We got the family wagon tonight." Rob was wearing his drummer sweatshirt, light tan Levis cords and blue Adidas tennis shoes and he smelled as fresh as a bar of soap. "Head down Lakewood Boulevard to the Traffic-circle bud," he said, "the party's at Chuck Turner's apartment, on PCH near Sambo's restaurant."

"Who's Chuck Turner?" I asked, and Rob turned to me with a surprised look.

"You don't know who Chuck Turner is? Jeez, he's only just a drummer legend!" Rob rolled down the window and hung his elbow out. "He was one of the most bad-ass tenor drummers that Concert Band ever had! He quit the band a year ago, but I figured you would have heard of him by now...he's the dude that taught Karl and Greg how to play tenor drum." I shifted in my seat, taking in this interesting piece of drummer history. "He got married and had to leave LBJCB," Rob continued, "but we totally surprised the hell out of him and played drums at his wedding. Imagine the shock of seeing a line of drummers in full uniform on either side as you walk out of the church doors, cranking out cadences as you head for the limo...it was so righteous! Anyway, he's moving out of his apartment this weekend, relocating out of state," Rob continued, "so he's having a drummer party before he hands over the keys...you know, last chance to thrash the place before he's out of there. It's a real drummer tradition!"

Jeff hadn't told me about Chuck Turner or about the drummers playing at his wedding, but I made a mental note of everything Rob was telling me since I would be meeting this 'drummer legend' tonight. "Bro, you've got to start remembering the names of the legends," he continued, "Chuck, and then there's Jim Black, another famous tenor drummer...and also Walt White who became the best drum major that LBJCB ever had!" I made more mental notes as we jammed straight down Lakewood Boulevard heading south towards the Traffic-circle. "Don Kelly, Larry Muzinski, just to name a few," Rob continued, "but these are the guys that actually wrote a lot of the first drum cadences...they're the forefathers of our drum section." As I approached the Traffic-circle my hands gripped the steering wheel tighter because I knew from past experience that this loop of curving lanes with cars all merging together was dangerous...it connected Lakewood Boulevard, Pacific Coast Highway and Los Coyotes Boulevard in one massive circular flow, and it was no place for a greenhorn driver like me.

"Maybe we should go another way," I said to Rob, even though it was already too late to turn around.

He replied sarcastically, "What, can't you handle the Traffic-circle? Come-on man, don't be a wimp...just go for it!" Telling myself that I would not be called a wimp driver by a non-driver like Rob, I leaned forward and began planning my entry. Looking to the left, cars were speeding toward my lane to merge over to northbound PCH, and to the right, more cars raced down PCH to curve around onto Los Coyotes going east. Somehow I needed to end up on PCH driving southbound towards Chuck's apartment.

"Okay then, don't blame me if we die," I said, and nervously covered the brakes of the Olds wagon, slowing down at the 'yield' sign. There was a solid flow of cars speeding by so I stopped, waiting for a break in the traffic. I finally saw an opening and hit the gas, praying that we would live to see the drummer party.

"Holy shit! Rob yelled, "You're going in too fast, truck on the right!!" I slammed down on the power bakes causing the wheels to chirp and the rear of the wagon to lurch upward. I nervously looked to the left and right to see what Rob was yelling about, but it looked clear.

"Quit messing with me!" I yelled, thinking he was playing another one of his tricks. I somehow merged the wagon over to the right, but still needed to get one more lane over if I was going to wind up on PCH. Just as I got to the far right lane and was about to yell at Rob again for making jokes, I saw the red semi-truck barreling down the southbound PCH lane right towards us. The driver hit his horn, "BLAM-BLAAAMMM!" and Rob and I both jumped, screaming, "Mother Frick, We're Dead!!!" I swerved to the left and punched the gas pedal to the floor like a survival reflex, jolting the wagon forward. Luckily the horsepower of the 350 engine kicked in, leaving the Mack truck in the dust.

Straightening the steering wheel and easing off the gas pedal, we were out of danger and back to cruising mode, ending up right where we needed to be heading southbound on PCH. "Boy, I thought you were shittin' me for sure," I said nervously, "how did you spot that truck before me?"

"Christ," Rob exhaled, still holding his hands up to his forehead. "That was close dude...how could you miss a bright red Mack truck coming down PCH like a frickin' locomotive?!"

"I don't know, it just came out of nowhere...and like I said, I thought you were just BSing me like always!" I replied.

"Hey, I *do* not and *will* not joke while we're on the Traffic circle," Rob said, pointing his finger at me, "especially when we're about to get creamed!"

"Well did you ever hear the story about the boy who cried wolf?" I snapped back, and could see Rob glaring back at me, shaking his head with his arms crossed.

"Yeah-yeah, but that's just bull. Maybe I do joke too much sometimes, but I figure you of all people should know the difference by now...anyway, forget about it. Just look for a Sambo's restaurant somewhere on the right. That's where the guys are meeting before we go in." About a quarter mile up the street on the right I could just make out a cluster of guys in brown drummer sweatshirts standing in a parking lot. I hit the turn signal indicator and the green arrow clicked in the dashboard as I moved over to the right and then pulled the wagon into the Sambo's parking lot.

The drummers were in their usual huddle next to their muscle cars, the brown and gold sweatshirts looking like some kind of 'gang' colors, as if to signify a bunch of teen hoods looking for trouble. I could hear the familiar sounds of cussing and laughing and the smell of cigarettes as I pulled the wagon into a parking spot right next to a cool looking green Ford Pinto. Although the words 'cool' and 'Pinto' usually didn't go together, I had to admit that this one had actually pulled it off. It was slightly jacked-up in back with slotted U.S. mags that had a dull silver finish, and a nine foot whip CB antenna extended straight up from the rear bumper. Mark McMullen climbed out of the Pinto and started unscrewing the CB antenna from its base and I had to chuckle to myself, thinking, *Man, the drummers even trick out their non-muscle econo-cars!*

When the guys spotted me and Rob they all turned and gave us a long look. I could see their lips moving as they exchanged comments and snickered among themselves and I started getting nervous again, wondering what Rob was getting me into. Rob and I stepped out of the car and I tried stuffing my Mom's bulky key chain into my pocket, but with no luck. She liked to keep her keys together in one dangling mass like a school janitor...said they were easier to locate in her purse that way. I removed just the car key and hid the rest in the glove compartment. I then locked the car door and dropped the single key into my front pocket, then reminded Rob, "Make sure to lock it. You have to hold the knob in."

He looked at me and shrugged. "Okay-okay," he said, and he slammed the door shut.

We walked over to the drummers and I immediately recognized Tom, Greg, Dave, Mark, Joe, Gary, Rick and Lonny. They were all chuckling about something and then Rick Spiegel turned his attention toward us. "So you decided to bring the peon trainee with ya, heh Wubbie?" he blurted out, making the other guys giggle. Rob nodded his head and started shaking hands with a tight grin. "This must be a drummer first," Rick continued, "inviting a trainee. Sure hope he can handle it." I stood there with my hands in my pockets, clutching my Mom's key, not sure what to do or say next.

Rob covered my ass, saying, "No problem boys, Bri here can handle it."

Scott Peterson chimed in, "Well, if he can handle a bunch of drunken drummers giving him shit, then he can handle just about anything I guess."

Mark McMullen nodded his head in agreement and said, "Fricking-A right, welcome aboard trainee...prepare to fetch my beer!" and he gave me a drummer handshake. I exhaled, realizing that his was about as warm a welcome as I was going to get.

Lonny also shook my hand and said, "Just remember one thing trainee...never trust a drummer." Every one chuckled and I wondered what the hell kind of warning Lonny was giving me.

Just then the 'bruised banana,' Gregg Sciotto's yellow Chevy Camaro pulled into the parking lot with a squeak of its suspension and the low rumble of its 396 engine commanding attention.

"Cool, Gregg made it," Tom said, as the street machine whipped around fast, its chrome Crager wheels shimmering as Gregg cranked the wheel and pointed the car directly towards us. He revved the motor up so loud that the car sounded like a beast ready to pounce. Then he popped the clutch making the car lurch towards us, and we all jumped back as Gregg came within inches of our knees before making a hard right and gliding the car neatly into the parking slot next to Dave's Coronet. I could see Gregg's devilish grin through his handlebar moustache as he killed the engine.

"Son-of-a-bitch, Gregg!" yelled Tom, as Gregg stepped out of the car.

"Scared ya' didn't I?" Gregg said, sporting the same cocky grin. A couple of the guys flipped him the bird as he walked toward us, but Gregg just smiled and said, "Love ya' too boys," and started shaking hands. Gregg wasn't wearing his drummer sweatshirt, but instead was totally decked-out in fancy duds. He had transformed himself into something right out of a Hollywood movie…he wore a long tan camel coat with a fur-lined collar, red and blue plaid bell-bottom slacks and a white wool turtle-neck sweater. Completing the look, he pulled out a wood-handled pipe from his coat pocket, placed it between his lips, and lit it with a silver Zippo in one swift gesture. He puffed on the pipe and let the smoke escape from the side of his mouth, the thin white smoke swirling around his moustache and up through his perfectly trimmed curly brown hair. It filled the air with a real sweet cherry tobacco scent and I thought, *this is not the same Gregg Sciotto that played bass drum with us apes in the choir room at LBJCB practice!*

"Hey it's Broadway Joe!" shouted Tom, and everyone chuckled out loud. Gregg did look a lot like football star Joe Namath, but I hadn't noticed it until he showed up wearing those threads.

"Hey there Sciotto, you yankee-doodle-dandy!" shouted Dave in a very feminine voice, making us all crack up again. "Got an audition tonight in tinsel-town or something?"

Gregg seemed to love this kind of attention, and with two more puffs of his pipe he said, "Ha…sorry ya weenies, hate to disappoint you but I have a date in a couple of hours, unlike you guys. Just thought I'd grace this party with my presence for a little while before picking her up."

Gregg must have been a couple of years older than the rest of the guys and was definitely more sophisticated. He had more style in his pinky finger than any of us goofballs. We looked like a bunch of hobos standing next to him.

"Hey McBride, glad you could make it," Gregg said, and he shook my hand. "Don't let any of these clowns screw with you, and if they do, just tell me and I'll kick their asses!" This brought on more loud snickers, but Gregg had a way of making you feel good, especially if you were a trainee. Other guys just ignored the trainees, but Gregg always came up and shook your hand, asked how things were going. I heard some of the drummers razzing Gregg about his attendance, saying that he was more interested in chasing pageantry girls than playing his bass drum. Guys were starting to call him 'Sciotto the shadow' and 'the phantom.' I didn't know if this was true or not, but I thought he was just a really cool guy, even if his style didn't quite fit the image of the hulk-like bass drummers. Earlier, Rob had told me that Gregg already had one foot out the door and would be quitting LBJCB soon, but might come back as a band chaperone. This one made me laugh...imagine an ex-drummer as a band chaperone? No doubt he would get an immediate assignment to watch the drummer bus.

We stood waiting for the man-of-the-hour Chuck to get here so that he could let us into his empty pad and get the party rolling. Sure enough a faded blue 1970 Chevy Impala four-door pulled up and the guy inside rolled down the window and said, "Far out guys, thanks for waiting...some of you hop in, but the rest of you just run across the street to the carport over there, and I'll park it and show you into the place."

With that Sciotto yelled, "Shotgun!" and jumped into the front seat, while four more guys ran for the back doors, yelling "Seniority!" They scrambled into the back seat just before Chuck hit the gas, the doors slamming shut as the loaded car bounced over the curb and jammed out across PCH in a plume of nasty smelling smoke.

Pacific Coast Highway was several lanes wide and dangerous to cross on foot, but I didn't see any cars coming on either side so I took off running as fast as I could with the rest of the drummers. Half a dozen guys sprinted across PCH illegally, jaywalking all the way to the other side. We joined the others at the carport and Chuck led the way down a sidewalk and around to the front lobby of the apartment building. "It's on the third floor, follow me." Chuck said, pointing the way. Guys were goofing off and making noise, but Chuck let out a "Shhhh!" and everyone piped down as he pulled on the big glass door. It swung open with a dreadful scraping sound and I noticed that the lobby looked pretty much thrashed. It had stained blue carpeting, a sagging brown and gold couch, and a fake plastic plant in the corner that hadn't been dusted off in years. There was a musty smell in the air too, and the hallway leading to the elevator had taken quite a beating. There were jagged scrapes and gouges all over the wallpaper from years of careless tenants moving their furniture in and out of the building.

"Must be a reasonable rent in this place, heh Chuck?" said Dave with a sarcastic smirk, as we all stepped into the lobby. The other guys tried to hide their laughter, but it came out in suppressed bursts.

"Oh you're real funny Geopforth, a real card," Chuck replied calmly, seeming more than familiar with snide drummer remarks. "Why do you think I'm leaving this rat-hole anyway?" He said, as he walked up to the elevator and pushed the 'up' button. "It was fine when I was single, but now..." I could hear the clunking sound of the worn-out motors rumbling from inside the thin walls. "The wife and I need a bigger place...got a much better situation up in Portland, Oregon," Chuck continued, "better jobs, lower cost of living, and a much nicer place to live. Hope some you boneheads will come up and party once we're all settled."

Tom nodded and said, "Hell yes we'll visit, as long as the beer is flowing!"

The elevator doors creaked open, revealing dark brown paneling with the same battle-scars as the lobby. "Everyone cram in!" said Chuck, and twelve guys started squeezing into the small space. I was the last one in, and Chuck reached under my arm to hit the '3' button and the doors slid shut within a quarter of an inch of my back side. An image of frat boys piled into a telephone booth entered my mind as guys pushed, shoved and cussed at each other all the way up to the third floor. The elevator stopped with a jolt and we all spilled out to the dark hallway.

Chuck led us down the hall to apartment number 30, and he swiftly opened the door with his key and said, "Now don't you bastards thrash the place too much, or I'll never get my deposit back!"

CHAPTER 9

We stepped into the apartment one-by-one and I glanced across the empty and dark living room. To the right was a small kitchen with a grey Formica counter-top, and beyond that was a hallway which I guessed must lead to the bedroom. Dave started unraveling the power cord of a portable stereo that I somehow hadn't noticed he was carrying, as the other guys spread out through the rest of the apartment flipping on light switches. Chuck walked across the living room and pulled open the drab white curtains of the sliding glass door, revealing a gloomy back-alley view at nighttime.

"Sam's on his way with the brewskees," Chuck said as he turned and looked around. Chuck had a thin build and wasn't much taller than me, but his forearms were huge just like the other tenor drummers. He looked like a hippy from Woodstock with his curly brown afro hair, long sideburns, and a thick moustache that barely hid the deep lines of his face. He wore Wallabee shoes, faded bell-bottom jeans and the oldest looking drummer sweatshirt I had seen. It had even more stripes on the sleeve than Lonny's. His fingernails and calloused hands were stained with black grease and I figured that he must like tinkering with car engines.

Chuck noticed me standing there, and gave me a look as if I had just appeared out of thin air. "Who are you?" he asked, and I had that self-conscious feeling again, realizing that I was finally meeting Chuck Turner, the drummer legend.

"Brian McBride, tenor trainee," I replied, and Chuck's eyebrows lifted as if totally surprised.

He sneered and then stared straight into my eyes. "A TRAINEE? Who the hell let you into this party, anyway?" he demanded, and I figured the jig was up and he would be kicking my ass right out of there.

"Rob needed a ride," I replied very quickly, figuring the truth was probably the best way to go, "so I offered to drive him here and the guys agreed that I could come along if I kept my mouth shut and served beers." Chuck nodded slowly and didn't say a word at first. I held my breath and stood there, petrified. Finally his face relaxed and he actually grinned, as if satisfied by my answer. "Well, at least you know your place, trainee." He said, then took four steps toward the kitchen area and flipped on a light switch. "How many tryouts so far?" he asked, and I exhaled. Guys were talking and laughing in the other room, oblivious to our conversation, which was a lucky break.

"Just had my first one last Sunday. Next one is in ten days." I replied.

Chuck crossed his arms and began stroking the whiskers of his moustache with his fingers. He seemed to be contemplating what to say next, his steely eyes staring right into me. Finally he pointed his index finger right into my chest. "Good. You'll try out for as many times as it takes...until you're worthy," he said, as if getting something off his chest. "No more of this 'pushy' crap." he continued, "Did you know that there was actually a time...a while back ago in '74, when Marvin would actually force us to vote trainee's into the section if he thought tryouts were taking too long?" I nodded my ignorance to this information. "He'd do it mainly just before big performances like Shrine or Vegas, to build up the drum section. Not that this was a bad idea mind you, having fourteen snares and all...but most of those trainee's just weren't ready yet." I continued to nod as I listened, fascinated by what I was hearing. "Well anyway, we called any trainee that got in that way a 'pushy' because they didn't get in by a legitimate drummer vote. It was an insult to be pegged a pushy...but finally Marvin realized that it just wasn't working, so he gave us back our drummer voting rights."

Chuck was rambling on but I was absorbing every word, totally intrigued. This was the drummer history that I knew wouldn't be coming from Rob or Jeff...it was back before their time. I was glad to hear that the 'pushy' days were over. Even though it might mean four, six, or even eight tryouts for me, at least I would never have the humiliation of being labeled a 'pushy.'

Chuck continued, "Marching in the tenor rank will be harder than you can imagine kid," I didn't interrupt him to mention that I already had some first-hand experience. "It's a real test of physical strength and willpower...finding the stuff inside of you that gets you to the end of that parade route." I could tell by the look on Chuck's face that he had been there many times before. "It's an awesome feeling though...the conquest of making it to the circle-up after a God-awful summer parade, playing cadences in uniform on hot asphalt with your drummer brothers." Chuck looked towards the kitchen at a cluster of drummers, then at the doorway where more guys were standing, and his eyes seemed to water up with emotion. "I've marched many, many miles with these guys...we've been through a lot. They played drums at my wedding last year...and I'll be damned if they don't end up playing at my funeral some day when I'm dead and gone!" Chuck then gave me a drummer handshake that almost crushed my fingers, saying, "Good luck, McBride. You'll need it." He released my hand and walked over to the kitchen with the other drummers. It felt like the passing of some kind of drummer torch between Chuck and me...a hand-off between the old and the new.

I spotted Rob waving me over from across the room and followed him past the kitchen and down the short hallway. There we found a bedroom and connecting bathroom, both completely emptied of furniture and personal items. The apartment was in the same sad shape as the lobby, with stained beige carpeting, dingy walls and the smell of cigarette smoke.

"Well it doesn't look like much," Rob said, "but it's perfect for a drummer party, that's for sure."

"What do you mean by that?" I asked.

"The less stuff in the house, the less stuff that gets thrashed by wasted drummers," Rob replied. "Come-on, let's see what's going on in the kitchen."

Just as we walked back into the living room Sam came busting through the door and slid a case of beer down from his shoulder onto the kitchen counter. McMullen shouted, "Its Miller time gentlemen!" and everyone hooped and hollered as they reached over each other for a cold beer. Dave grabbed a beer and then leaned over his stereo and cranked up the volume. I immediately recognized, *Nights in White Satin* by the Moody Blues. He twisted off the beer cap and flung it across the room, then swigged the beer with one hand while reaching in his back pocket for a plastic Wiffle-bat with the other. Making a *Whoop!* sound with each swipe of the bat through the air, he yelled, "I'm gonna nail any drummer that gets out of hand with my nischy-stick!" I stood next to Rob near the hallway and didn't make eye contact with Dave, in hopes that he wouldn't single me out as the only trainee in the room, and *whoop* me just for the hell of it.

It didn't take long for the drummers to start showing signs of inebriation. Guys were spread throughout the living room, hallway and bedroom, talking more and more loudly with bursts of hysterical laughter becoming more frequent. Chuck, Sam and Greg were standing in the kitchen, talking noisily as they chugged down beer. When they heard the stereo, they all broke into song, shouting like drunken pirates, "NIGHTS IN WHITE SATINNN... NNEVER REACHING THE ENNND!"

Rob turned to me and said, "It's starting to get frickin' crazy man...hey Bri, go ahead and have a beer. I'm sure the guys won't mind at this point."

I hadn't really intended to drink at all since I had Mom's car and knew that I had to get it back in one piece. I'd only been to one other beer bash in my freshman year and I couldn't even finish half a bottle of the bitter tasting stuff back then.

"Naw, that's okay, I'll just watch for now." I replied halfheartedly, still thinking of my Mom's car. I had to admit it though, I was curious to try it again, especially since the drummers seemed to be having such a blast.

"Ah come on...just take one and nurse it." Rob prodded, "Then you won't draw attention for being such a teetotaling lightweight."

He had a good point. I could at least hold one beer bottle all night and pretend that I was pounding them down. "Well all right, guess I'll try just one."

With that Rob quickly stepped across the room, grabbed two bottles of Miller High-Life and popped off the caps with a church key. "Cheers!" he said and handed me the chilled beer. We clinked bottles with a mutual nod and took a long cool swig, feeling like real men all of a sudden. The icy-cold fluid slid easily down my throat this time, not as bitter as the first time I had tried it. I took a couple more swigs and felt a warm sensation flowing straight through my chest, followed by a pleasant rush of dizziness directly to my brain. I had to admit that it felt pretty damn good. All of the tension in my body instantly melted away and I felt relaxed for the first time all night.

"Glad you made it, Bri," Rob said.

"Thanks for inviting me. This is really cool," I replied, and took another chug of beer. Rob seemed pleased to have successfully gotten me into this party, as well as the whole drummer scene for that matter. I looked across the room at all of the brown and gold sweatshirts...guys drinking and smoking and laughing their butts off, and I envied them. They were already in the exclusive drummer 'club' while I still had so far to go before I would be accepted. Even though I was standing inside of the drummer world drinking their beer, I knew that they wouldn't give me the time of day until I proved myself on tenor drum and got voted in.

Just then Tom Masterson walked up to us with two freshly opened beers in his hands. He must have been at least three beers into the night already as he said with a slur, "Heyy McBride, let's see who can pound a beer the fastest, whadda-ya say traineeeee?"

Rob and I looked at each other, and since I didn't have the slightest idea how to react and Rob knew it, he quickly chimed in, "Hey, pick on someone your own size. I'll take you on, bro!"

Tom stared at me with glazed eyes and I knew that I had to say something in my own defense. "I would like to," I replied lamely, "but I have to drive my Mom's car home in a couple of hours and..."

Tom snorted at me with a disgusted look and said, "What a wussie trainee... Wub, I guess it's just you and me then." With that Rob grabbed one of the beers from Tom's hand and stood straight up facing him. They both raised their beers and tilted them to their mouths as if they had done this before. Rob shouted, "Ready... GO!" and both guys started chugging the beer down as fast as they could. I could see both Adams-apples moving up and down as the beer went straight down their throats. Beer started spilling out of the sides of Rob's mouth, but he kept guzzling it down and the bottles were emptying out like Sparkletts water coolers.

Although Rob was the bigger dude, Tom was obviously more experienced at this, because he beat Rob by a good second. He slammed the bottle down onto the carpet, which spared it from shattering into a thousand pieces, and then let out a huge belch. "BRRRAAAAAPPP... Now that's what I call victory!" Tom shouted, and wiped his mouth with the sleeve of his drummer sweatshirt. Rob finished his and then mimicked Tom by throwing his bottle to the floor as well, causing it to bounce once, completely flip up in the air, and then clink right next to

Tom's bottle. Rob may have lost the drinking contest, but he would have definitely won a belching match, because he let out the loudest, longest burp I had ever heard in my life! It was so loud that you could hear it over the stereo... Rob actually talked through the belch saying, "Eeeat-myyyy-shoooorts-Tooomm!" Every drummer stopped talking and turned their attention to Rob, and then they all started laughing and shouting, "Nice... Way to Go Wub!" I was laughing so hard that I had to lean against the wall just to keep from falling over. I took another long chug of beer, savoring the nice buzz flowing over my entire body and the craziness of it all, as the drummers continued to get more blitzed.

As the night went on, the stereo got louder and so did the drummers. The beer was flowing endlessly and things were getting more and more out of control. I kept in the background as much as possible, sipping my beer and walking from room to room, observing the whole event like a fly on the wall. Occasionally a drummer would yell, "Hey trainee, beer me!" and I would run a fresh one right over to him. I had to chuckle at the hilarity of it all, thinking, *Wow, so this is a real drummer party.* Some high school parties I heard about involved smoking pot, but these guys didn't seem to need to touch the stuff. In the kitchen five guys were chugging beer and smoking Swisher Sweet cigars, arguing loudly about how the last part of a cadence called 'Lori' should be played. They were really serious, pounding it loudly on the counter top with their fists, interrupting each other and almost push fighting over it. Several other guys stood in the living room, arm-in-arm in a circle singing, "BEEN DAZED AND CONFUSED FOR SO LONG IT'S NOT TRUE..." as Led Zeppelin blasted from Dave's stereo speakers. *These guys are sure into music,* I thought, and realized that this made perfect sense considering they were all drummers in a marching band. *Another reason that I like these dudes,* I thought, feeling relieved that I wasn't the only geek totally hooked on music instead of sports. I couldn't wait to tell Jeff what he was missing out on.

I walked down the hallway into the bedroom looking for Rob, and detected trouble when I found him sitting in the corner holding his head. "What's wrong man?" I asked.

Rob rocked back and forth with his head down, not saying a word at first. Finally he muttered, "Think I drank the last one too fast... I'm getting the spins." Not knowing how to help him, all I could think of to say was, "That sucks dude...toilet's right over there if you need it."

Rob replied in a very low voice, "Great...that's just great Bri, thanks. I know where the toilet is."

Even though it was only ten o'clock, looking at Rob's condition made me think that we should bail out of the party and get him home right away. "I'll go check things out and be right back," I told Rob, and he nodded back, still holding his head between his knees.

I walked back into the living room just in time to see Dave whack Rick Spiegel on the backside with the Wiffle-bat.

Rick spun around in surprise, "What the hell did you do that for, Dave?" he yelled, rubbing his pants with an irritated look. Dave swung the bat towards Rick again, but stopped just short of hitting him.

"Psych!" Dave said with a sarcastic grin when Rick flinched. "Take a wild guess, man?" Dave pointed his 'nischy-stick' over towards the kitchen counter. "Look at all those beer bottles Spiegel...none of them're empty! I count three bottles that are still half full," Dave swung the bat towards two more bottles leaning against the wall on the carpet, both also half full. "Look over there on the floor by the patio...and what's that in your hand?" Dave asked, and Rick looked at the unopened bottle he was holding.

Rick then looked up at Dave with glassy eyes. "So what, so I like 'em fresh and cold...what's the big frigging deal?"

Dave shook his head back and forth, smacking the bat in his hand. "What do you think, ya dufus? I've been watching you for the past hour...you're WASTING OUR GADDAM BEER!" The other guys stopped talking and listened to hear what Rick would say next.

Sam chimed in, "Yeah, quit wasting the frickin' beer Spiegel...it's easy, just finish a whole one, put the bottle in the trash, and then start a new one, in that order."

Greg Golson picked right up on the sarcasm, saying, "Yeah, considering that you only pitched in two dollars for the beer, I'd say...let the rest of us have some, okay bud?" Guys started laughing at Rick, but he just shrugged his shoulders, realizing that he was outnumbered in this particular argument. "Tisk-Tisk," Greg continued, "just look at all the half-empty beers...look at all of the Spiegel-beers!" Everyone busted up when they heard this, and they all started chanting, "SPIEGEL-BEERS! SPIEGEL-BEERS! SPIEGEL-BEERS!"

Rick's face turned bright red and he shrugged his shoulders again with his arms raised, saying, "Hey give me a break you a-holes...those aren't all mine!" He flipped everyone off with both hands and then took off running down the hallway into the bedroom. Dave yelled, "You can run but you can't hide, Spiegel!" as he swung the bat overhead and chased after Rick. I could hear the bathroom door slam shut, then some loud thumps that shook the whole apartment, and then some screams and cussing followed by some very loud whacking sounds. Dave had apparently discovered that the bathroom door didn't lock.

The drummers had a very short attention span and quickly resumed their partying while Rick took a good-humored beating. I was just glad that the attention wasn't on me. Glancing across the room I noticed that Tom was standing alone in the small dining area, right under a low hanging lamp where the kitchen table was supposed to be. He looked pretty drunk and was staring at the glass lamp and mumbling something to himself. He then started to hop up and down, dancing around the lamp like a boxer. He started swinging at the lamp like it was an imaginary punching bag, and he kept barely missing it with his fists.

I cringed with each swing of his arm, knowing what would happen if he connected with that glass.

Sam must have read my mind because he shouted at his older brother, "TOM! Watch the lamp…you're going to bust it!"

Chuck was in the kitchen and hadn't noticed Tom until he heard Sam yelling. Chuck shouted, "Dammit Tom, get away from there! If you break it they'll take it out of my security deposit and then I'll have to take it out on YOUR ASS!"

This was just enough to distract Tom, and sure enough as soon as he looked towards Chuck, one of his fake punches connected with the lamp. The cheap, thin glass shattered everywhere, flying onto the carpet and all over Tom's arms and clothes.

"Holy Crap Tom!" yelled Chuck, "Now you clean that up!"

Sam shook his head and said, "Holy Shit, brother! Do you really WANT to go to the hospital?!"

Tom staggered backward with a bewildered look on his face, as pieces of glass fell from his shoulders. "Oh…damn," he whispered, his drunken mind realizing what he had done.

McMullen yelled, "Way to go Masterson…we'll send you the bill!" and the other guys started cheering and whistling loudly.

Chuck shouted, "Everyone stay away from the glass…can someone help pick up the pieces?"

Figuring this was something a trainee was expected to do, I said, "Sure, I'll do it."

Chuck nodded in my direction, saying, "Thanks McBride, just throw the glass in this trash bag over here." I squatted down and started picking up the larger pieces of glass, stacking them carefully in the palm of my hand. Tom was staring at his hands and seemed oblivious to his surroundings, his body swaying back and forth. Then he noticed me hunched over the broken glass and he leaned down to show me something.

"Wow, check this out," Tom said, and I could see the cut on his right hand. It was a deep slice right between his thumb and forefinger. Amazingly, it wasn't bleeding yet, so you could see the flesh just under the skins surface. Tom must have been so numb that he couldn't feel any pain, because he started pulling the cut apart like he wanted to examine it closer or something.

"Gross, dude!" I said and quickly looked away.

Tom saw my reaction and shouted, "BA-HA! Can't handle it, can ya traineeee?"

He giggled and held his hand up closer to my face trying to taunt me, but I stepped back and said, "Hey watch it...it's gonna start bleeding!" He looked at his hand again and saw blood trickling out, and his expression turned blank. His face turned white as a sheet.

"Oh man, I think I'm going to pass out," he said and headed for the hallway holding his injured hand up in the air. I watched him stagger into the bathroom and then slam the door so hard that the walls vibrated.

The party was getting more out of control and it was showing no signs of slowing down. Some of the guys wanted to make another beer run and started taking up a collection for beer money. Chuck protested to anyone driving, so Sam convinced the guys that there was a 7-Eleven that they could walk to. They took off walking down the hallway towards the elevator, obviously wasted. They were singing some really weird version of the Twelve Days of Christmas at the top of their lungs. The rest of the drummers were still head-banging in the living room, the stereo cranked up full-blast to the keyboard sounds of Emerson, Lake and Palmer.

The apartment was thrashed, totally littered with beer bottles, cigar butts and fast-food wrappers. There were bottle caps strewn about everywhere and streaks of beer running down the walls. *How the hell did beer get on the walls?* I thought. Someone had brought in a stack of Playboy magazines and they were scattered about everywhere on the floor. One guy was sitting in the corner reading one, turning the pages slowly. There was a thick fog of cigar smoke in the air and it reeked of stale beer and human sweat. It was enough to make you want to hurl, but the drummers didn't give a damn…they were having a royally bitchin' time. Some guys were shirtless and dancing around the living room in a tribal circle, while others played air-keyboard and screamed out the lyrics to 'Karn Evil 9.' It was a raging teen male frenzy and I wanted to jump right in there with them. I loved the way they partied with the same unrestrained passion as when they played syncopated drums.

My one-beer buzz was quickly fading though, so I decided to go check on Rob and Tom. I found Rob sitting in the exact same spot on the floor of the bedroom, with Tom sitting next to him holding his wounded hand. He had wrapped several layers of toilet paper around it, but you could still see blood seeping through the thin tissue.

Tom looked up at me with blurry eyes and a drunken grin. He said, "Hey man…when Sammy getz back, tell him I need-er-rride home will ya traaineee-ol'-buddy-ol'-pal?"

I nodded and said, "Sure Tom, no problem," I looked at his wadded up hand again, "maybe Sam should get you to a doctor too…looks like your hand is still bleeding pretty bad."

Tom stared at his hand and mumbled, "Naaaw…just need to cleeen id-up-a-liddle-bit…put a bandage on iz-all."

I turned my attention to Rob, saying, "How you doing, Wub? Can you get up?"

"Shirrr, no problemo!" he said and attempted to stand up, but he staggered sideways and I had to grab his arm just to keep him from falling.

"Woah, easy there bud," I said, using all of my strength to hold up his tall frame.

"I think I'm going to puke," he blurted, and by the look on his face I knew that he wasn't joking.

"It's right over there. GO!" I said anxiously, pointing to the bathroom door. He leaned forward and took three lumbering steps towards the bathroom. He disappeared behind the door and I could hear him drop to his knees at the toilet with a thump. The next thing I heard was Rob going into a fit of dry-heaves.

The choking finally settled down and I could hear Rob catching his breath. It was silent for a few seconds and then he began mumbling into the toilet bowl, "Help me Mister Wizard, help...I don't want to be drunk anymore...please make the spins go away...help mister Wizaaard!" Even though I felt bad for Rob, I couldn't help but chuckle at his line from the old 'Tooter the Turtle' cartoon. I peeked my head into the bathroom and chanted, "Drizzle-drazzle-dradle-drone, time-for-this-one-to-come-home!" Rob wasn't completely gone, as I could hear his muffled giggles echoing from within the toilet bowl.

Rob was sitting on the floor straddling the bowl, his hand holding the toilet seat up and his head resting on the porcelain bowl. I noticed blood smeared on the toilet seat just above his head. "Hey man, are you bleeding?" I asked, pointing to the toilet seat.

He slowly lifted his head and gazed at the raised seat, then nodded left and right and replied, "No way man...not mine."

Then I realized that Tom had just been in there cleaning up his cut hand. "No worries Wub," I said, "it's frickin' Tom's blood. He busted the kitchen lamp and gashed his hand."

Rob let out a faint chuckle. "Tom's always doing shit like that," he said, "jeez, even in an empty apartment he finds stuff to break."

Just then Mark McMullen poked his head into the bathroom. "Hey, what kind of gaiety is going on in here?" he said with a smirk. I pointed to Rob's slumped body.

"Rob ain't doing too good," I replied, "he just puked."

Rob lifted his head and said, "I'll be fine, guys. Just let me sit here for a few minutes."

Mark's eyes darted around the bathroom and then he noticed the blood on the toilet seat. "Holy shit, did Wubbie just puke up blood?"

Realizing the mix-up, I tried to explain, "No man, it's not Rob's blood, it's..."

Before I could finish Mark shouted, "Hey guys come over here, Sainburg just puked up BLOOD!"

"Screw you man, it's not my blood, it's TOM'S!" Rob yelled, trying to get up on his feet. I stepped towards Rob to help him stand up as more guys crowded around the bathroom doorway, trying to get a glimpse.

"Wow, look at that," Gary said, "Do you need us to call you an ambulance, Wub?"

This seemed to agitate Rob even more, and he yelled, "Shut up man, NO...it's Tom's blood, not mine!"

Dave peeked in and studied the situation with a less-than serious expression. "Hey what the hell's going on in here?" he asked sarcastically, then lowered his voice and said, "Well doctor, seems that we have a case of bleeding hemorrhoids...nurse, give this man an enema and then call me in the morning, we'll have breakfast." The guys huddled behind Dave were laughing like hyenas and Rob seemed to be sobering up fast in his frustration.

"You guys totally suck!" Rob yelled, "For the last time, it's NOT MY BLOOD!" He started pushing his way through the drummers as they whistled and cheered.

"Come on Wub," Greg said, trying to grab Rob's arm, "We're just messing around. Relax...have another beer!"

Rob pulled away from Golson and I followed him through the crowd of heckling drummers. Sam and the others had returned from their beer run and Sam was hovering over Tom, trying to wake him up. "Come on brother, time to get up," he said while slapping Tom's face, but Tom was out cold and snoring loudly.

Rob and I made it to the living room just as someone yelled, "There's another Spiegel-beer over here boys...let's get the bastard!" We made it to the front door and just as I opened it, Rick ran past me and out the door as fast as he could. A second later six drunken drummers rushed out the door and down the hall, chasing after Rick and yelling, GET BACK HERE SPIEGEL!"

Ten seconds later I heard the loud thumping of feet coming toward me from the hallway as Rick tore past me again, running back into the apartment. Rick was breathing heavily as he ran towards the bedroom, but he was stopped short by Chuck, who made a surprise attack. He tackled Rick onto the living room floor just as the drummers came racing back inside. Rob was leaning over the kitchen counter next to me, and we both watched as Chuck and Rick wrestled on the floor, Rick yelling, "You ain't gonna get me Turner, you son-of-a-bitch!"

Then someone shouted, DOG PILE!"

Rick was actually holding his own against Chuck until Greg, Sam, Gary, Mark, Dave and the others all jumped him, burying Rick under a pile of sweaty bodies. It was like they were initiating him all over again. They were laughing hysterically as Rick covered his head with his arms, shouting, "Get off of me, you fags!" but it was no use. Three more guys jumped on top and all you could hear was laughing, slapping and grunting.

Then Mark McMullen came running full speed from the hallway and he took a flying leap, landing on top of the heap of drummers, yelling "BANZAI!"

"Let's get out of here Rob," I said quietly, wanting to get back to the safety of my Mom's station wagon.

"For sure bro, you lead the way." Rob said, and we headed out the door. I took one last look at the apartment...at the beer-stained walls, the broken glass and debris strewn everywhere...the tangle of sweaty drummers piled right in the middle of it all...and I just had to laugh.

Rob mumbled, "Man, poor Spiegel never had a chance."

I closed the door behind us and thought, *Man, neither did Chuck's poor apartment!*

CHAPTER 10

I woke up Saturday morning feeling energized, having slept like a log after my one-beer buzz at the drummer party the night before. I felt good about getting my Mom's car home on time, even though I knew that the only reason we left early was because Rob had gotten sick at Chuck's party. I figured that I was doing a whole lot better than he was this morning, as well as the rest of the drummers for that matter. The way they were partying last night, I wondered how they could pull it together to play drums at Knott's Berry Farm this afternoon.

I had to laugh at everything I had seen the night before...what a classic! Laying there on my bed, I stared at my aquarium and picked at the calluses that were forming on my hands. I thought about how hilarious the drummer party was...how totally out of control, with beer bottles flying, broken glass thanks to Tom, and Dave's nischy-stick. *Spiegel beer,* I thought amusingly, and then finally got up to brush my teeth. I showered, combed my hair, and with a shot of Right-Guard under each arm I got dressed in standard 'trainee' attire...faded tan Levis cords with a brown leather belt, a plain white t-shirt tucked in, and a pair of beat up suede blue Adidas with white stripes. Grabbing my beige Catalina Martin jacket, I headed to the kitchen for breakfast before heading out to pick up Rob and Jeff.

"Hey Bri, how was the party last night? Mom asked in her usual cheerful way, as she stood near the sink in her robe pouring coffee into her mug. My Dad had already left early to attend a dental convention, but I figured I'd get a chance to chat with him later on.

"It was really fun," I replied, once again leaving out the funky details of the drummer underworld that somehow just didn't seem fit for a mother to hear. "Those guys are cool," was all I said, as I reached for the box of Frosted Flakes in the cupboard. Visions of beer chugging contests flashed in my head as I shook the cereal box, watching the sugar-coated flakes tumble into the bowl. I could hear the TV blaring in the den and knew that my little brother Darren was still lying on the couch in his pajamas, his eyes glued to Saturday morning cartoons. The familiar, "Poink-Poink... Tee-Tee-Tee-Poink!" sound effects of Bugs Bunny reruns still cracked me up...they were etched in my memory from watching those same episodes a thousand times.

"Today will be fun," I said, as I poured milk over my cereal, "I'm picking up Rob and Jeff and driving them over to the Arby's on Spring Street...that's where the band buses pick everyone up. I'll get to ride on the drummer bus and then watch the band march through Knott's Berry

Farm in front of hundreds of people." Dipping my spoon in the cereal bowl, I took a large mouthful and kept talking as I chewed, "It's opening ceremonies for a new ride at Knott's called the Parachute Sky Jump. I can't wait 'til I get into the drum section Mom... I'll get my red drum and uniform and be able to march down the street wailing for the crowds...it's gonna be so bitchi'...er-um, awesome!"

Mom let out a small giggle. "Just be patient, Bri," she said as she opened the refrigerator and took out a package of Farmer John bacon. "You're really a good drummer. I'm betting that you get in the next time you try out." I finished wolfing down my Frosted Flakes and then rinsed the bowl and set it in the sink.

"I sure hope you're right, Ma," I said, and grabbed the keys to the Olds wagon from the brass hook marked 'Keys' on the wall above the telephone. "Thanks for letting me use the car again," I said, and gave my Mom a peck on the cheek and headed for the back porch out to the garage. "I'll see ya later today, and I promise to bring the car back in one piece."

*　　*　　*

"Step on it, Bri," Rob said as I pulled the wagon out of his neighborhood and headed down Del Amo towards Jeff's house. "We've still gotta pick Jeff up and it's already quarter to ten. If we're late we'll not only get chewed out by Marvin, but we won't get good seats on the drummer bus!" Being paranoid about getting a speeding ticket, I was driving at exactly the speed limit, which only made Rob more impatient. "Come on man, punch it!" he demanded, and I shot him a look that said *chill out!* "Okay-okay I'm just saying...hey, take Paramount to Carson, not Cherry...it's faster." Rob said, and he was pointing out the window and being a total control freak as always. I had to admit that he was right about taking Paramount Avenue though, so I followed his suggestion and drove past Cherry and hung a right onto Paramount.

"Hey you're the one that forgot his band shoes and made us have to turn back, dude," I said defensively. "Ain't my fault if we're late." Rob looked down at the white band shoes that were sitting on his lap. He quickly put them on the floor.

"Yuk!" he said, "You don't know how many times I've stepped in horse crap in these shoes at parades. Guess I'm not quite thinking straight since the party last night. Anyway, can't march without 'em, so we had to turn back, all right?"

He was wearing his drummer sweatshirt, black Converse tennis shoes with red socks, and his band uniform pants...royal blue with red and gold stripes stitched down the sides. He looked pretty put together considering he had been puking his guts out the night before. "I should know better," he continued, "we're supposed to do a mental checklist before every performance." He turned to look at the shako box and plastic garment bag that he had thrown in the back seat. "Let's see, shako, uniform coat, belt...drum strap and suspenders...white gloves, sticks, and tape...extra t-shirt and pants for the bus ride home, feather plume to be issued, drum is on the truck... I think that's about it."

Turning left onto Carson Street, we headed towards Jeff's house near the VA hospital. "You forgot one thing," I said, and Rob turned to me with a puzzled look.

"What?" he said, taking me seriously for a second.

"Isn't it obvious?" I replied, trying to be sarcastic, "You forgot your brain...it's still at Chuck's apartment!"

I pulled up to the curb in front of Jeff's house and he immediately appeared, hopping into the back seat holding the same shako box and garment bag as Rob's. He was wearing the same get-up...drummer sweatshirt, blue band pants, red socks and he already had his white band shoes on.

"Hey brother-dudes, what took you so long?" I glanced at Rob to indicate that *he* should be the one to answer that question.

"Never mind," Rob replied. "Between my absentminded brain and slowpoke driver over here, you're lucky that we made it at all. Now let's get the hell over to Arby's!"

* * *

Rob and I told Jeff all about Chuck's party, and he seemed to get a real kick out of hearing about the beer chugging, broken glass, and the dog pile on Rick Spiegel. "Classic drummer bash," he kept saying, "what a rager...next time I'm there for sure!" We finally turned onto Spring Street and in the distance I could see the four yellow school buses parked along the curb in front of Arby's. I pulled the wagon into the parking lot and cruised past a collection of bandos, pageantry girls and band staff all lining up in front of the buses. The girls had on their gold pageantry sweatshirts, white uniform skirts and curlers in their hair, while the guys all wore their blue uniform pants and different colored sweatshirts, depending on what instrument they played. I saw red for tubas and blue for trumpets...and of course brown for the drummers, which is the direction I pointed the car to find a parking space. The drummer cars were parked on the far side of the Arby's lot and I immediately spotted Lonny, Dave, Karl, Greg, Mark, Rick and the others. I pulled the wagon into a nearby slot, shifted it into 'park,' pressed the emergency brake with my foot and then cut the engine.

From a distance someone yelled, "Let's Go! Everyone on the buses!" and I realized that it was Marvin Marker. The drummers seemed to be ignoring this at first, but then slowly started moving towards their cars to grab their gear. Rob and Jeff hopped out of the wagon with their stuff, and I rolled up my window and then made a circle around the car to make sure that all of the doors were locked.

"Thanks for the lift Bri," Rob said.

"Yeah thanks little bro," Jeff added, and we headed towards the fourth bus.

Walking past the familiar Arby's building shaped like a covered-wagon, the neon cowboy hat sign rising overhead, we got in line to board the drummer bus. Rob was looking all around and seemed distracted. I figured he was trying to see if his girl Dena had gotten there yet. "If we're lucky we'll get a seat towards the back," Rob finally said, "back of the drummer bus is the best spot...more drummer privacy, especially with the girlfriends if you catch my drift, but a lot of guys pull seniority, so we'll see." I didn't have any preference of where to sit, I was just glad to be sitting on the drummer bus at all. I glanced across the parking lot toward the other buses and watched as dozens of teens lined up at the bus doors, their boxes and bags in hand. The adult staff, called 'chaperones,' stood at the foot of the doors, chatting casually with the bus drivers as people took turns stepping onto the buses. The drummers and their pageantry girlfriends had formed a line behind me, Rob and Jeff. I thought, *Funny how the drummers are always in the back...back of the band, back of the parking lot, back of the bus...yet they're also the backbone...the back-end powerhouse of LBJCB!*

"Out of my way, trainee!" shouted Rick Spiegel, and he pushed his way past the three of us and hopped onto the bus. This caused a chain reaction as the rest of the drummers started pushing and shoving past me, mumbling, "Excuse me, pardon me trainee...seniority... excuse me, pardon me...seniority!" They all took cuts as their girlfriends giggled and followed them right up the steps of the bus.

"Sorry little bro," Jeff said with a grin, "but like Rob just said, drummer seniority kind of rules around here, and let's face it, you're at the bottom of the totem pole which puts you at the front of the bus."

Just then Rob's girlfriend Dena ran up and gave Rob a peck on the lips. Like the other girls, her brown hair was up in curlers and the makeup on her face made her cheeks so red and eyes so large that she looked like a marionette doll. "Hey, sorry I'm late," she said as Rob grabbed her box and bag, his arms now totally piled up with all of their band uniform stuff.

"It's okay, Deena-leena. You're actually just in time, but let's hurry or else we'll be stuck up at the front of the bus." With that I stepped aside as Rob and Dena walked past me and onto the bus, Rob whispering with a smirk, "Excuse me, pardon me...seniority...just kidding Bri, see if you and Jeff can get a seat near me and Dena."

"Looks like it's just you and me little bro," Jeff said as he picked up his items and stepped into the narrow doorway of the bus. "You're just lucky I'm not going steady with anyone right now, or you'd be S-O-L. Come-on, let's go." I followed Jeff up the four steps into the bus and realized that it was full and we were the last two people to board. The bus doors slammed shut behind us with a hiss.

I glanced past Jeff all the way down the center aisle of the bus looking for an empty seat, but did not see any. *Is this some kind of trick...where the hell are we supposed to sit!* I thought, feeling self-conscious about being stranded in the aisle-way. No one was paying attention though, as the drummers were too busy stowing their gear or trying to open the sliding glass windows, while their girlfriends chatted away with each other. I looked around for Laura but didn't see her. *Boy it sure would be great if she were here so I could maybe sit with her,* I thought, and figured she must still be feeling pretty sick to be missing a band performance. Just then I heard the hiss of the bus door opening again, and up came Sam Masterson. His face was flushed and he was breathing hard like he had been running.

"Hey, Sammy, we were wondering if you'd make it!" Gary Erbe shouted. "Work another morning crew shift, did ya?" Sam glanced at Gary and rolled his weary eyes.

"Yep, midnight to nine, right after the drummer party." Sam replied and then barged past me and Jeff looking for a place to sit. "Almost thought I was gonna have to drive to Knott's." Rob had told me that Sam put in a lot of hours working the graveyard shift as a night clerk at Ralph's grocery store. Rob said that Sam often marched parades after working all night with hardly any sleep. I was amazed that he could do all that, plus make a drummer party. "Tom's out though," Sam continued, "ten stitches on the hand...all bandaged up, can't hold a snare stick." That one didn't surprise me. What did surprise me was that everyone else looked fine. There were no signs that the drummers had stayed up late the night before, pounding down beers at Chuck's party.

"Hey, Sammy, back here!" yelled Rick, and Sam made his way to the back of the bus with gear in hand, then plopped down on the bench seat in the very back. *Total seniority move,* I thought, as the doors slammed shut again and the bus started rolling forward. I followed Jeff slowly down the aisle hoping we wouldn't have to stand all the way to Buena Park.

Jeff stopped half way down the aisle and said, "Well, it don't look like we're sitting together little bro, but here's two end seats. I'll sit next to Ron and you can sit back here next to Wally." That was all right with me because Wally was cool, but Ron didn't seem to like the idea of sitting with Jeff at all.

"Hey no way, man," Ron grumbled, "I need my space!" He then raised his legs up onto the seat.

Jeff stood there holding his gear, glaring at Ron in disbelief. "What got your panties in a bunch this morning, dude?" he said, shrugging his huge shoulders.

Just as I started to sit down next to Wally, Lonny shouted, "Hey Malave, just for that you get to sit with the trainee today. Jeff you go sit with Wally... Ron, move your ass out of the way for McBride!"

The drummers started chuckling and one guy yelled, "Yeah, put the trainee next to Ron...that'll cover his initiation!" I looked at Jeff and waited, wondering what to do next.

Ron got up from his seat and shouted, "Hey, you guys suck! I always get stuck with the trainees!"

Then someone yelled, "That's right Malave, if a trainee can handle a bus ride with you, he deserves to be in the section!" Another round of chuckles as Jeff sat next to Wally and motioned me over towards Ron.

"Hey come on Malave, be cool," Jeff said, "that's my trainee you're talking about. McBride here's a cool guy. Besides, it's your chance to tell him what you know. Teach him all about...drummerhood!"

Then someone heckled, "Yeah, teach him how to chew on his chin strap while playing drums during a parade!" Guys were laughing and throwing gum wrappers at Ron, but he just shrugged and started flipping everyone off with a grin. He seemed to actually like the attention, and I realized that this making fun of each other was just another form of drummer bonding.

Ron plopped back down in his seat and then looked over at me. "Come on trainee, have a seat." He gestured for me to sit and I did. "Hey nothing personal McBride, but these jerks just give me non-stop crap about everything is all. I get a little edgy sometimes."

"No problem, man," I said, "just a bummer that the bus is so full."

Then Ron looked me over with a sly grin and put his hand on my leg, saying, "That's not a problem trainee, as long as we can be...friends."

I shoved Ron's hand off my leg and yelled, "You're gross, dude!" Ron giggled hysterically at my reaction, and I realized why Lonny had put me here...he wanted to see just how much I could take. Ron seemed to be a more than willing accomplice.

He leaned his head on my shoulder and fluttered his eyes, saying with a goofy girlish voice, "Ah come on...give a lonely guy some company." I pushed on his shoulder as hard as I could, but the more I pushed the more it made him laugh. I realized that this was going to be a very long bus ride.

The buses rolled steadily in the slow lane along the 91 Freeway towards Knott's Berry Farm, but it was too slow for me considering that Ron needled me the whole way. Every few minutes he would pinch my arm or lean his body into me, and I'd yell, "Cut it out!" while he giggled and the guys in the back snickered.

Finally Ron said, "Don't worry McBride, I'm just messing with your mind. We just want to see that you can take some crap like a good trainee, but not too much...you know, push back some too. That's the sign of a good drummer. You're doing fine." I didn't really follow the logic, but was glad to hear that I was somehow passing his strange trainee test.

Then I heard a girl's voice in the seat in front of us saying, "Hey, Ron, why don't you leave the poor guy alone? He's gonna think you drummers are all just a bunch of freaks." I looked up and saw that two pageantry girls in gold sweatshirts had turned to face us. The girl talking had wavy brown hair, fair skin with freckles, and was really cute. The girl sitting next to her...well, she was the most beautiful blond I had ever seen in my life!

"I wouldn't be wasting my time with this trainee if you'd

ever come sit back here with me Sandi," Ron said with a wink of his eye, "what do ya say...you game?"

Sandi rolled her eyes and replied, "Not in a million years, Ronny boy."

This brought more chuckles from the back of the bus, and someone shouted, "Hey Ron, why don't you stop asking her and just go ahead and *moose* her?!"

I wondered what the hell that meant, to 'moose' a girl. I made a mental note to be sure to ask Jeff about that later.

Ron shrugged his shoulders and looked at Sandi. "It's your loss, honey," he said, "ya just don't know what you're missing."

Sandi ignored Ron's comment and looked at me and held out her hand. "Hi, Brian, I'm Sandi Werner and this is my friend Teri Schweitzer."

I shook Sandi's hand awkwardly and said, "Hi, Sandi."

Then I made eye contact with Teri and the butterflies in my stomach went into overdrive. She was a stone fox. Her face was beautiful...perfect lips, nose, and brown eyes outlined by silky blond hair that looked gorgeous even with the curlers. She could have been Barbara Eden's double in 'I Dream of Jeannie.' I didn't know what to say next, but then Teri said, "Hello Brian," and held out her hand. We shook hands gently and I felt her soft fingers, and then realized with total embarrassment that my hands were clammy.

"Hi Teri," I said, kicking myself for not thinking to wipe my hand on my pants.

"Nice to meet you, Bri," Sandi cut in, and then leaned towards me and whispered, "Teri won't admit it, but she told me earlier that she thinks you're really cute."

The next thing I heard was the unmistakable "Swack!" of an arm being slapped. I watched as Teri flung her hand up again, ready to take another swing at Sandi, screaming, "What did you say to him... Werner, what did you say?!" Sandi blocked Teri's second attempt with her hand and was wincing through her mischievous giggles.

"Oouch...just for that I'm never telling," Sandi said, and then stuck her tongue out at Teri. She then turned around and plopped back down in her seat. Teri looked at me, her face flushed red, and then covered her face with both hands before sinking down behind the seat.

I could hear Teri complaining, "Oooh, you little witch, Sandi, I'm *never* riding on the bus with you again!" The bickering between them continued and I couldn't stop grinning.

*   *   *

The buses finally pulled to a stop along the backside of Knott's Berry Farm and when the rumbling of diesel motors stopped, everyone started unzipping their garment bags and getting into their uniforms. Ron needed room to get dressed, so I stood in the aisle and tried not to stare as the pageantry girls quickly pulled off their sweatshirts and put their red uniform jackets on. Then I saw the top of Marvin's head passing by the bus windows and heard his voice through the megaphone, "Okay, people now listen up. I want everyone in band formation and ready to go in ten minutes...ten minutes to full band formation!"

This brought on groans from all around, and someone mumbled, "Yeah right, it's just another hurry-up-and-wait situation as always."

I watched as guys hurriedly buttoned their uniforms and gave their band shoes another coat of white Kiwi polish, while pageantry girls held compact mirrors up to their faces trying to apply yet more makeup as frantic activity swirled all around them. Jeff walked up to me and looked ready to go with his shako in hand and taped-up fingers.

"Hey Bri, just stay close to me today," he said. "I'll have you follow behind us with Jack when we march, and you can be a runner...you know, help Jack pick up dropped sticks or fix a drum if someone busts a head or snaps a snare string." That sounded like an okay job to me, even though I really wanted to just strap on a drum and march down Knott's Main Street in uniform, playing cadences with the drummers.

"No problem, just tell me where to go," I responded, and reminded myself to just be patient...some day I'd be a drummer and have my own trainee assistant. "By the way," I said, remembering my question for Jeff, "what's this moosing thing? Is it the same as *goosing* a girl?"

Jeff's eyebrows lifted and he let out a loud hoot. "Oh dude, that's a riot!" he said, and started chuckling uncontrollably. "Sorry...we're just so used to saying it, but I guess it's not very self-explanatory, is it?" Jeff finally recovered from his laughter and then put his hand on my shoulder. "Sorry little bro, I shouldn't expect you to know these things...it's just, I've never been asked about that one," he said. "The word 'moose' is just a silly name the drummers came up with...it's our code word for French kissing!"

That was the strangest word for kissing that I had ever heard. I pictured a large-lipped moose and it kind of made sense in my head, but just barely. The drummers had a bizarre sense of humor at times. It took some getting used to, but it could also be quite entertaining.

I stepped out of the bus with Jeff and we walked over to the band trucks. I watched as the band started lining up in ranks and files just as it did every week during practice. This time, however, LBJCB was in full 'Technicolor,' each person adorned in the dazzling red, royal blue, and majestic gold of the LBJCB uniform. *Wow, they've all transformed into living, breathing toy soldiers,* I thought, as I watched a staff member hand out gold feather plumes that attached to the top of the shakos. This added the final touch to the uniform, giving the band members more height, which created a massive presence when combined with the tall flags and shields. The rolling LBJCB banner was wheeled to the front where the drum major and baton twirler stood, and it also looked impressive. It must have been ten feet wide by four feet tall and it rolled on a metal base that had three spoked bicycle wheels. Three pageantry girls pushed it from behind and it was cool to watch the mechanical louvered face change every few seconds…the slats rotating first to read, 'Long Beach Junior Concert Band' in red letters, and then flipping to read, 'Hello Knott's Berry Farm!' in blue letters.

The band assembled near a huge wooden gate that no doubt opened to Main Street on the other side. The gate and wall that surrounded Knott's Berry Farm was built in the same 'logged fortress' old frontier theme as the rest of the park. The drummers crowded around the back of the equipment truck, calling out their drum numbers one at a time as Jack hustled the drums down. My heart ached with envy as I watched each drummer clip on his shining red sparkle drum and head towards his position in the drummer ranks.

"Hey Bri," Jeff shouted, "when we start marching, just go wherever Jack goes."

I nodded and walked over to where the drummers were standing in the very back. Jack was still handing out drums in the truck, so I just stood by the drummers, waiting for the next thing to happen. It was fun to be 'behind the scenes' at Knott's for the first time. Marvin and several LBJCB staff members stood next to a couple of Knott's employees with walkie-talkies, obviously discussing the sequence of events for the day. I knew that as long as the wooden gate was closed, the band wasn't going anywhere, so I kept that gate in the corner of my eye. I didn't want to be left behind when the band stepped off and watch the gate closing in my face, some Knott's security guard telling me, "Sorry, only band members allowed beyond this point."

The day was sunny with clear skies and a cool breeze...perfect conditions for marching a parade. The pageantry girls unraveled their flags and got into their 'V' position in front, making the band appear even more magnificent as the flags waved proudly in the breeze. The scent of fresh popcorn filled the air and I could hear the familiar overlapping bass-murmur of distant music coming from inside of the theme park. I spotted Teri and Sandi walking towards the front of the band, balancing their tall flags vertically in leather holsters as they continued their conversation. Teri looked foxy in her red jacket and short white skirt with matching white boots. *Man, whoever designed those pageantry uniforms knew what they were doing,* I thought, and took another long look at her slender legs gracefully outlined by the knee-high boots. Just then I heard the familiar whistle-blows from the drum major and knew that he was about to take charge of the band.

"BAND...stand at, EASE!" he barked, and the light tapping of drums, blowing into instruments to warm up the chops, and general chattering all stopped. He then shouted, "BAND...READY!" and two hundred sets of feet all snapped together. My feet came together like a reflex with the rest them, and I yearned to be standing with the drummers in full uniform, tenor drum on, and mallets crossed at my face. I couldn't wait to watch the reaction of the crowd as the drummers unleashed their first cadence...to see that same look on their faces as I'm sure I had that first night at Vet's Stadium.

Marvin's megaphone clicked on. "Okay people, the gate will open any minute now," his amplified voice continued, "Jeff will step you off with OBST, then Freedom Fanfare...a set of drum cadences and then right into Tribute-to-Troy." The megaphone clicked off and Marvin nodded towards Jeff the drum major, who then made eye contact with Lonny, who then turned his head toward the drummers.

"Drummers listen up," he said, "the set will be Roll Cadence, Candy, Hendrix-swing and then right into the Tribute intro. This is it boys...let's kick some ass!"

The Long Beach Junior Concert Band stood alert and ready, waiting for the next command. Jack Bowen walked up to where I stood next to the drummers. He was fully equipped with extra snare sticks, mallets, and rolls of tape protruding from his back pockets.

"Can I carry anything?" I asked Jack, wanting to be useful.

Jack looked at me and said, "Nope...thanks anyway Brian, but if you'll just follow behind and watch for dropped sticks, pick them up and get 'em back to the drummers, I'll cover the rest."

I gave Jack a thumbs-up and then glanced across the ranks of the drum section...they all stood as still as statues, their serious expressions in direct contrast to the image of a crazed dog pile that I had witnessed the night before. Now that I knew my job, I stood and waited, wondering how much longer it would be. I didn't have to wonder for very long, because the wooden gate started to slowly swing open. Marvin clicked his megaphone on again, saying, "Okay, this is it." The gate finally came to a complete stop, revealing the familiar old west interior of the Knott's Berry Farm that I knew so well as a kid. A crowd of hundreds of people lined both sides of Main Street, and a voice broadcasting from the park's intercom system announced, "And now folks, a parade of music and pageantry in the finest Knott's family tradition, celebrating today's main event...the grand opening of our newest attraction, the exciting new Parachute Sky Jump ride!" A guy with a walkie-talkie gestured to the drum major, and with four sharp chirps of his whistle LBJCB stepped-off into the park like a Trojan army.

The band had a tradition of yelling a chant called *Our Band Sticks Together* at the beginning of every parade. Rob called it the 'OBST psych-up,' and as the band stepped off the drummers clicked off the four counts into it. Since I had learned it during practice, I shouted it as loud as I could along with the band to the cheering Knott's crowd.

"OH!" click-click-click "BE!" click-click-click "ES!" click-click-click "TEE!" click-click-click "OH!" click "BE!" click "ES!" click "TEE!" click "O-B-S-T, RAH!!"

The drummers played the roll-off, the instruments went up, and the brass section belted out Freedom Fanfare.

Then the drummers kicked it into Roll Cadence perfectly and I was right in the jet-stream behind it all, taking in the awesome energy of the music, thunderous drums, and roaring cheers from the crowd. With chills running up and down my spine I marched proudly in back and kept an eye out for any dropped drumsticks as the drummers flailed away. The grin on my face would not go away and I didn't care... I was feeling 'OBST' more than ever, even as a lowly trainee. This was the most awesome marching band in the world and my whole mission in life was to get voted in and march in uniform for the Shrine show. My next tryout was coming up in a few days, and before I could even think about a blond named Teri or a brunette named Laura, I had to concentrate on mastering the tenor drum. I needed desperately to show the drummers that I was worthy of wearing the brown and gold sweatshirt and the LBJCB uniform.

CHAPTER 11

The days after the Knott's performance were intense with activity, as Jeff subjected me to his accelerated version of our daily routine, or 'trainee boot camp' as we called it. I drove him everywhere in the McGoo mobile while he relentlessly quizzed me on each drum cadence, hand signal, and proper sticking motion. I did more push-ups and chin-ups than I could count at Hartwell Park too, and Rob even filled in when Jeff wasn't around. He'd tap out cadences with me in his Mom's living room, showing me how the snare and tenor parts worked together, which really helped. By the time my second tryout came on Sunday February 22nd at Vet's Stadium, playing tenor drum felt more like second nature than ever before. Still, even though I had reached a new level of confidence, I also knew that it didn't mean squat if I couldn't hold it together in front of the drummers. That was the real test. I prayed that I wouldn't fall apart under pressure when the time came.

Practice ended that Sunday afternoon after three solid hours of rehearsing for the Shrine show. Marvin had the band go through the stage sequences over and over until the bandos couldn't blow into their instruments anymore and the pageantry girls couldn't do one more high kick in the chorus line. At four o'clock the band was dismissed and Lonny once again kept the drum section in place while the band packed it up to leave. He announced my name and also a new guy named Jeff Loomis, a snare trainee, as the two tryouts for the day. My stomach tightened again when I heard my name, and I realized that the nerves weren't going away no matter how prepared I felt. I took comfort in noticing that the sky was cloudy and the breeze was cool, so I wouldn't have the sun beating down on me during my tryout. *I'll take any advantage I can get in the endurance department,* I thought, and tried to relax, taking in deep breathes while I waited.

Lonny dismissed the drummers to sack up their drums, but asked Charlie Villegas, Rick Spiegel, and Wally Masterson to play again for my tryout. He also asked Karl to play tenor for Jeff's tryout. "To save time let's do the tryouts right here," Lonny said, pointing to a spot right along the chain-link fence that surrounded the stadium parking lot. "McBride, you'll go first. You stand right over there a few feet away from that fence, facing the fence."

The guys sacked their drums and walked back from the equipment truck, spreading out along the chain-link fence. I walked over to my spot in front of them, crossed my arms, and looked straight ahead. Over their shoulders I could see the spot right under the crooked oak tree where my first tryout took place. I thought about all that I had seen and done as a trainee just since then...everything leading up this day. This was the moment of truth.

Jeff walked up to me and shook my gloved hand, saying, "Good luck, little bro. You know what to do. We've covered it a hundred times. Now just dig in and go for it!" Rob came up right behind Jeff and said, "Right…just give it your best shot Bri. Think Shrine show!"

I stared straight ahead and tried to clear my mind. Even though the words from Jeff and Rob gave me encouragement, the nerves were creeping up on me fast. I knew that I had to control them if I was going to survive this tryout. I focused inward and tried to ignore the presence of the heavyweights standing in front of me…watching, listening, and judging.

"Come on, guys!" Lonny yelled out to the stragglers at the band truck, "let's hustle back here and get these tryouts done!" The mass of brown and gold standing in front of me grew wider…their eyes and ears alert, ready to size me up. The fear began its paralyzing grip and I took more deep breathes, closed my eyes, and fought back a wave of panic. Call it my Catholic school upbringing, but a prayer entered my mind in that moment. *Please God, just let me show them what I know without blowing it…give my arms the strength…help me to make it to the end of this tryout, still standing on my own two feet.*

Just then I was taken completely by surprise when Laura Villegas ran up to me, reached over my drum, and gave me a hug. "Good luck, Brian," she said, "I know you'll get voted in today. You're a great tenor drummer." I couldn't believe my eyes, Laura was right here all of a sudden. I hadn't seen her in over two weeks!

"Laura!" I said excitedly, "where'd you come from? Are you alright?"

She smiled and pulled a red bandana from her coat pocket. "This is for good luck," she said, and stuffed it in my back pocket. "I'm feeling much better now, thanks. I had something called mononucleosis. The doctor said I couldn't go to school or band practice since I was too contagious. Not contagious any more though." I gazed at her silky dark hair pulled back in barrettes, her warm smile, and her beautiful brown eyes and thought, *I'd catch mononucleosis from you any day of the week, Laura Villegas.* "I'm bummed that I missed Knott's and the practice today," she continued, "but I made my Mom drive me here just so that I could wish you good luck. I'll be back to band practice next week for sure!" I couldn't believe what I was hearing. *Laura came down just to see me,* I thought, my face feeling hot all of a sudden.

"Thanks Laura," I said, "it's really great to see you...and I'm glad you're feeling better."

She gave me a wink and started walking back towards her mother's idling car. "See ya next week, Bri!" she said, and then jumped in the car and waved at her brother who was standing behind me. "Bye, Charlie!" she shouted, and off they drove towards Clark Avenue. I stood there with drum and mallets, awaiting my trial, watching Laura's car drive off in the distance, and a new surge of confidence filled my heart. Her visit was just the boost I needed to get me through this tryout.

"You done with the funny business, McBride?" Lonny said, taking his position directly in front of me. I nodded and stared straight ahead, my body stiffening. Lonny waited until the rest of the drummers quieted down. Then he shouted, "Drummers...at EASE!" and the tryout ceremony began. I stood with my head down in 'at ease' position, bringing my full attention back to the drum. Charlie whispered from behind me, "Good luck McBride, let's do it." and I responded with a slight nod. Lonny then shouted, "Drummers...READY!" and the four of us snapped up at attention. Lonny nodded to Rick, then threw the first hand signal...it was rim beat. He raised his snare sticks high and clicked off four sharp cracks that echoed loudly through the stadium. Rick started right on cue with the rim clicks and I bounced lightly on the tenor drum, playing the low rumbling cadence. Lonny threw the signal for one-through-five next, and I closed my eyes and waited for the snare intro, determined not to screw it up this time.

My mallets came down on the drum with precision and volume, answering the snare intro and then gliding right into the first part of one-through-five. Although I was a nervous wreck I felt less confused about the cadences than before, my brain somehow relaying the tenor parts to my arms without a hitch. The breeze hit my face like a good omen and I raised my arms higher, digging into one-through-five. I was still on a high from seeing Laura. Feeling the lump of the red bandana in my back pocket, I took her positive energy and threw it into the drum. I hammered down the rest of the one-through-five, then Lonny called Hendrix-swing, and I played its demanding lead tenor part better than I ever had. Lonny threw the next hand signal and it was Linda, the tenor cadence I had totally blown during my first tryout. I knew this was Lonny's obvious attempt to start breaking me down, but instead of panicking, I thought, *Yeah Lonny, come on...bring it on you bastard!* I plowed into Linda like a madman.

Lonny must have seen the defiance in my eyes, because he called Linda again, and I heard someone shout, "Here we go trainee, let's see if you can take it!"

I looked upwards toward the sky and then over to Jeff. I gave mental thanks for all of his help...the non-stop cadence drills and ten thousand pushups in the park. It was surely going to help me now. Jeff stood there with his fists up like he was at a boxing match, shouting, "Come on McBride! You can do it!" I ignored the burn in my muscles and kept digging in, pounding out Linda again as if my life depended on it. I worked to control my breathing, repeating, *In through the nose, out through the mouth,* as beads of sweat began trickling down my face, back, and legs. Although I played Linda perfectly, Lonny was relentless, throwing out more hand signals, one after another... Linda into Candy, Sally into foot, roll cadence into lefty...but somehow I kept holding it all together. It wasn't until somewhere between roll cadence and lefty that I hit the wall. My arms had lost steam and my mind was starting to slip. I was entering into that delirious fatigue that had become so familiar, yet that I dreaded more than anything. *Not yet,* I repeated to myself, refusing to show any sign of slowing down...desperate to keep on playing.

I looked out at the faces of the drummers, every set of eyes bearing down on me, and as I struggled to raise my arms to play roll cadence, something in my mind snapped. Everything suddenly went into slow motion. In my extreme fatigue both time and space became distorted and I went into some kind of a trance. I had never felt anything like this before, but it was like being transported to a different place...an ancient, prehistoric place. Lonny and the drummers became a blur and I entered some kind of alternate reality...my mind, body, and drum melding into one rumbling pulse. For a moment it felt like the heat of the jungle, like sparks rising from a tribal bonfire...the sound of my tenor drum casting its primal vibrations up to the sky, connecting with the primordial rhythm of the ages, transcending the suburban streets of Long Beach, and becoming my soul's timeless offering.

Like a bolt of lightning a renewed surge of energy flowed through my body. The gods had answered... I had found my second wind. As roll cadence ended and the first beats of lefty were played, the fatigue in my arms dissolved and a reserve of strength somehow kicked in. I took this strength and pushed past the wall, discovering that I could call upon new muscle power by sheer willpower...by my refusal to give up.

Using my whole body, I lifted my heels and reached for the sky with my mallets, bringing them down as hard as I could onto the drum. I let out the loudest yell of my life, screaming, "Aaaaaaaaaahhhhhh...!!! as all of the built up negative emotions inside of me were released...my hatred for the humiliation I endured in Catholic grammar school, my fear of the bullies on the playground, my loneliness and frustration toward the girls that ignored me...all of it, now purged through the drum. There it was, the truth...right there at Vet's stadium in the middle of my second tryout. I had a score to settle, a beef with society at age sixteen. For every bad experience that held me down...every childhood trauma that created the shy misfit named Brian McBride...the scared, weak and tongue-tied kid that I had become and was so ashamed of... I was now going to reclaim with each violent swing of my mallets onto the drum. The tenor drum would be my new voice, its violent fury creating an uproar in the world, sounding out a pure primal scream of released frustrations and declaring my new-found confidence with every ear-splitting, blood-boiling, fire-eating beat of the cadence! I didn't know if the drummers understood this, or anyone else for that matter...it didn't matter, this was personal. I needed to give everything to the drum, put my entire soul to it, not only for the pure love of it, but for my own salvation.

I snapped out of my trance, and to my complete surprise Greg Pepoy was jumping up and down, yelling,

"Go McBride...that's it, kick ass!" I was well into the second half of lefty, breathing hard and drenched in sweat. It was unbelievable, but true. The drummers were actually cheering me on! Instead of verbal insults, they were yelling, "Come-on man...almost there McBride...you're doing great!" As encouraging as this was, the end of my rope was near and I knew it. The backs of my legs were cramping from keeping my drum steady and I thought they might buckle under my own weight at any second. My body was shaking all over and I could feel the bleeding raw flesh of blisters on my hands underneath the gloves. I desperately fought to ignore the pain and maintain control of the drum as I finished off Lefty, thinking, *Ok Lonny you win... I may go out on a stretcher, but even if I collapse right now, I go home knowing that I gave it my best shot.*

Just as I braced myself for the big fall, Lonny shouted "Last one!" and gave the sweet, wonderful hand signal for Lucy, the last cadence of my tryout.

"BAM-BAM!! tat, tatta-tatta..." The first two beats of Lucy came down and I could hear Charlie, Rick and Wally breathing heavily behind me. "Come on Bri, let's wrap this up and get out of here." Charlie said, as Rick tapped the quiet snare part between the alternating loud beats. "BAM-BAM!! tat, tatta-tatta..." I knew that I hadn't played the most perfect tryout, there were a couple of screw-ups, one during Sally and another at the end of foot, but the rest was okay. I was just relieved that it was almost over. "BAM-BAM!! tat, tatta-tatta..." Standing in sweat-drenched clothes I struggled with mind-numbing fatigue, taking in deep breathes in an attempt to recuperate within the few seconds that Rick played the snare part. "BAM-BAM!! tat, tatta-tatta..." Charlie and I hit the two-beat loud part again and we were almost home-free. The memory was quickly fading, but I knew that for a few moments I had taken a glimpse into a powerful mystical world. Like a tribal sacrifice, I had offered myself completely in body and soul, contributed my own beat to the collective pulse of the universe, and in so doing felt more alive and connected than ever. My inner rage had been purged through the violent pounding of my drum, replaced with a calm that I had never experienced before. For me this was a kind of healing, and I was beginning to understand the true spiritual power of the drum.

"TAT-TAT-TAT—TAT-TAT-TAT—TAT—WAIL!!!"

I finished Lucy through a haze of stinging blisters, overstrained muscles, and wavering mental consciousness that was the unique blend of torture designated to a syncopated drummer. When it ended Lonny looked at me standing there, fighting to keep the mallets crossed at my face, struggling to resist the dull force of gravity that was pulling down on my arms. He nodded and said, "Not bad McBride, go sack your drum and wait by the truck... Jeff Loomis, you're up next."

I don't remember much of Jeff's tryout, being in a fog from my own marathon session, but I think it went pretty bad for him. He just wasn't ready to tryout yet and the drummers sneered and cussed at him until Lonny mercifully cut it short. I thought of my first tryout and felt bad for Jeff as he walked back to the trucks with his head down. I wished him better luck next time.

"Okay guys, that's it," Lonny yelled, "trainee's take a walk...drummers, meet at the truck and we'll vote." I walked away from the equipment truck and out to the vast empty space of the stadium parking lot, feeling the cold breeze against my wet clothes. Jeff Loomis sacked his drum and followed me to a spot nearby, then sat on the asphalt and began pulling on the weeds that were growing through the cracks. He obviously needed some privacy to mull over what had just happened to him. The drummers formed their tight huddle once again, becoming the voting committee that would determine our fate. I crossed my arms and looked up to the sky, wondering if I'd passed this time or would be preparing for my third tryout. O'Keefe had told me that most guys got in after three or four tryouts, but some guys had to repeat the grueling experience five or six times before getting voted in. That sounded like a long haul, but I knew that I would go all the way if I had to, even if it took ten tryouts. I was too tired to think that far ahead though. I just wanted to get the news and go home, drink a gallon of water, take a hot shower, and put some bandages on my sore hands.

After a few minutes the drummers broke their huddle and started walking towards us, with Lonny and Jeff in the lead. *Oh no,* I thought, *here it comes.* My heart started pounding in my chest and I became fixated on my possible failure. Even though I felt good about my tryout and guys had cheered me on, I had no idea if my playing truly met their standards when it came down to the final vote. Or maybe they just didn't like me...maybe I had said something stupid, looked at a drummer the wrong way, or done something wrong at Chuck's party. Maybe they weren't going to vote a guy in after just two tryouts no matter how well he played. Lonny came up to me and put his hand on my shoulder. I didn't like the serious look on his face.

"Brian," he said calmly, "it was a good tryout...a damn good effort." I braced myself for the bad news. "However, you just didn't get enough votes this time...sorry." My heart sank to the ground and my face burned with disappointment, but I tried to maintain and not show my emotions.

"It's cool, Lonny," I said, "next one will be better." Lonny shook my hand and then Jeff came up to me with a strange smirk on his face. I'm sure he knew how bummed I was by the look on my face. I figured he must be disappointed too since it was back to the drawing board for both of us.

"Well little bro," he said, and then gave me a bear hug that lifted me off my feet. "First rule to remember...never trust a drummer! Ha-ha-ha!" I didn't know what he was talking about. "Lonny was just BS'ing you man," Jeff said, "you're in!" I then saw the grin on Lonny's face and figured it out. I was in complete shock! "Unbelievable," Jeff said, "I've never seen it before...two tryouts, and everyone voted you in. It was fricking unanimous...way to go man!"

I suddenly felt bigger than life, totally elated. *My God,* I thought, *I'm an LBJCB drummer…a real fricking drummer!* Dave, Sam, Mark, Gary, Rick, Charlie and Greg…all of them gathered around and shook my hand, saying, "Good job McBride, welcome to the section…welcome to the brotherhood." Some started heading back to their cars while others took their turns congratulating me, and for a few minutes I felt like a real celebrity. Then Ron Malave walked up to me, shook my hand, and then whacked me in the gonads. I keeled over, waiting for the intense pain that follows. "First rule," he said sarcastically, "never trust a drummer." That line was really starting to get on my nerves. Fortunately the pain didn't come and I realized that he had missed…caught more of my leg than anything else. *Whew, not a direct hit,* I thought with great relief. I stood up and yelled, "Bastard!" and lunged at him. Ron dodged me and ran across the parking lot laughing like a hyena. I was too tired to run, so I let him get away this time, but decided to figure out a way to get even with him later.

"Dude!" Jeff yelled at Ron, "What are you doing whopping the guy, fool! Save it for the trainees… McBride is a drummer now…he's one of us!"

Karl Harkey came up to me next and he shook my hand firmly. "Never mind Malave," he said, "you did great…welcome to the drum section." He then handed me his drummer sweatshirt. "Here, wear this until you get your own." This blew my mind…it was like being handed the silver sword, like being accepted into the Knights of the Roundtable.

"Are you sure, Karl?" I said, looking at the sweatshirt, the three gold stripes sewn onto the sleeve.

"Damn right I'm sure...wear it in good health."

The smile on my face must have been permanently fixed...this was all too good to be true.

"Thanks, Karl," I said, "I promise to take good care of it."

Then Rob walked up and slapped me on the back, saying, "Just make sure to wash it before you give it back, Bri."

Karl laughed and said, "That sweatshirt has taken plenty of abuse...a little more drummer sweat won't hurt it." Karl shook Rob's hand and waved at both of us, then started walking towards his orange Dodge Dart. "See ya at next practice guys," he said, "don't do anything that I wouldn't do...and especially anything I WOULD do, ha-ha!"

Rob looked at me and said, "What'd I tell ya, eh? Isn't it the most bitchin' drum section around? I knew that if I could just get you to take one look..." Rob recapped the story and I remembered how resistant I had been until that day at the mortuary when I finally caved. Now I could hardly imagine that I almost hadn't agreed to come with Rob to see the drummers practicing at Vet's stadium.

"Yeah, you sure as hell were right about this one," I replied, "but I guess I just never got over sleeping in the mud at Camp Oaks in the pouring rain, in those leaky tee-pees...that was your idea too, you know."

Rob shrugged and said, "All right, all right, so I don't always get it perfect every time...but you have to admit I was dead-on this time. Now you're a full-fledged drummer and you're gonna be in the Shrine show!"

"That's awesome!" I replied, "Thanks, Rob...thanks for not giving up on me."

Rob nodded with a self-assured grin, saying, "Hey, it's no problem...what are friends for anyway?" He then looked over my shoulder and then back at me. "Looks like you're the new golden boy around here too...jeez, two tryouts and you're in like that...and now you've got two smokin' chicks after you. Here comes Teri Schweitzer now!" I turned around and sure enough Teri was walking towards us and waving. She moved like a fashion model, her silky blond hair shimmering in the sun, the breeze making it flow gently across her face. It reminded me of one of those slow-motion shampoo commercials. I was surprised that she had stayed for the tryouts. "Lucky bastard," Rob said to me as he waved back at Teri. "Oh well, that's my cue, I'm out of here. Karl's giving me a lift home so I don't need a ride. I'll catch ya' later." Rob ran to catch up with Karl while I watched Teri approaching. I tried to conjure up what to say without being overly enthusiastic, even though I wanted to shout at the top of my lungs that this was the best damn day of my life!

"Hey Bri," she said, "heard you got voted in. Congrats." She then threw her arms around my neck and gave me an unexpected hug. Suddenly my face was in her soft hair and I was breathing in her fresh, clean female scent. *Oh man,* I thought, *I'm in Heaven!*

"Thanks," I replied as she pulled away, "it's…it's just totally great." I didn't want the moment to end, but then realized that my clothes were sweaty and took two steps back. Pointing at my damp t-shirt, I said, "Sorry about the wet clothes, I should have brought something dry to change into."

Teri looked at me and smiled, saying, "It's no problem…comes with the territory. Everyone knows the drummers sweat more than anybody in the band. Personally, I kind of like it." There was something about Teri's straight forward attitude that I liked. "Hey, I wanted to ask you a favor," she said, "Sandi was supposed to be my ride home today, but she had to leave early, so I wondered if you could possibly give me a lift?"

Is it the brown and gold sweatshirt? I wondered, *is it really this powerful? It couldn't be just me, could it?* I decided to figure that one out later. "Sure…glad to give you a ride home," I replied, "let me just tell Jeff, since I'm dropping him off too." My stomach was churning…the butterflies were in full formation again.

"Great, thanks a lot Bri," she said, "it's not far, just a few minutes away…out towards Millikan High." She started walking towards the LBJCB truck. "I'll be right back. I have to get my coat…left it on the bumper of the band truck."

This was all new territory for me. Other than a first kiss with a girl named Maria after a St. Anthony's football game, I'd never had this kind of interaction with girls at school. Before becoming a drummer I was a nobody. Now I had a red bandana from Laura and Teri Schweitzer asking me for a ride home. I walked over to Jeff and told him about Teri.

"Primo, dude!" he said, "I'm totally jealous, but it's all good. I'll just sit in the back seat and keep my mouth shut."

The Olds station wagon was parked across the street from Vet's near the grass field of Long Beach City College. "Five minutes," I said to Jeff, and motioned for him to meet me there.

"Cool." he replied, and then glanced towards the drummer cars. "Looks like you're totally lucking-out as far as initiations tonight too, bro." he said, and I realized that I had totally forgotten about initiations in all of the excitement. My scalp tingled and I had a sudden urge to run to the station wagon, jump in, and lock all of the doors.

"Hey, what about Ron whopping me in the crotch, doesn't that count?" I asked jokingly, though wishing that it somehow did count towards my total initiation.

"Nice try, dude" Jeff replied with a smirk, "sorry, but that was nothing...just means that the guys don't have time tonight for some reason, which means that you get to look forward to a surprise attack when you least expect it!"

"Great...thanks for the warning," I said halfheartedly, now realizing that it would have been better if the drummers had just gotten it over with tonight.

The band truck was pulling out of the parking lot as the last of the drummer cars screeched off in different directions. As I walked across the street from Vet's stadium towards my car, a red Country Squire station wagon pulled up right along side of me and it was Marvin Marker himself. He rolled down his driver-side window and motioned me over. "Congratulations Mr. McBride, and welcome to LBJCB," he said.

"Thanks," I replied, and noticed Marvin holding up some forms.

"Here is an application to join Concert Band and also a map to Mrs. Lynd's house," he said, "you'll need to call her to make an appointment to get yourself fitted for a band uniform." This was the first time that I had actually met Marvin in person.

I took the forms and said, "Thanks Mr. Marker, I'll do that right away."

He shook my hand and said, "See you at practice on Tuesday, six thirty sharp. Welcome aboard!"

As his car pulled away Teri walked up from behind me and said, "My-my, getting the okay from the big man...aren't you special?" It actually *did* feel special being acknowledged by Marvin, like the King had just granted me access into his castle. I thought it was cool that he hung around after the drummer tryouts, just in case a guy got voted in. "Yeah, it's been a pretty wild day," I said, "you ready to go?"

Teri and I walked to the car and Jeff ran up to join us. "Hey, don't forget me kids. Hi Teri," he said, as I took the car keys from my damp pants pocket and unlocked the driver-side door. The sun had disappeared behind the Douglas airplane hangars and the cool night breeze was really giving me a chill. I realized that I had Karl's drummer sweatshirt thrown over my shoulder and quickly grabbed it and pulled it over my head. The sweatshirt was large on me, but it was dry and warm. I could smell Karl's spicy Avon aftershave.

"Looks good on you," Teri said, "so wow, I get to drive around with two real drummers."

I smiled at Teri and was about to open the driver-side door and jump in when Jeff whispered, "A-hem, aren't you forgetting something...it's girls first, dude."

Feeling like a total jerk, I quickly walked around the car to let Teri in. "Thanks Bri," Teri said and then stepped into the passenger seat. I slammed the door shut and gave Jeff a thankful nod as I ran back around to the driver's side and jumped in.

"Gotcha covered little bro, even though you're not my trainee anymore," Jeff said as he jumped in the back seat. "Hey drop me off first since I'm the closest." he said, and the two doors slammed shut. I fired up the Olds, flipped on the headlights and shifted it into gear, realizing that I had a lot to learn in the female department. *Still a 'trainee' in many ways,* I thought as I glanced at Teri Schweitzer sitting just inches away from me, running her fingers through her hair...that shapely figure under her gold pageantry sweatshirt and tan Dittos. I swallowed hard and felt the butterflies fluttering again. *You're in over your head McBride…just maintain,* I thought, then cranked the steering wheel around, pulled a u-turn, and punched it towards Clark Avenue and to Jeff's house.

The three of us exchanged small talk all the way to Jeff's house and I enjoyed the carefree thrill of having my tryout behind me and a pretty girl sitting in my car. I pulled up to Jeff's house and he got out, saying, "You did it, Bri, I knew you could…see you tomorrow morning before school." He tapped on the glass of Teri's window and said, "Bye-bye, Miss Schweitzer."

"See you at next practice, Jeffy." Teri replied with a wave.

I made eye contact with Jeff and gave him a thumbs-up, saying, "Thanks bro…for everything."

He shrugged as he walked up the path, saying, "Hey…what can I say, I'm just the greatest big brother of all time."

Teri let out a hoot, and I shouted, "Yah-yah, we know!" I hit the gas like a show-off, sending the car lurching forward faster than I expected. I could hear Jeff's howls as I hung on to the steering wheel, trying to keep the wagon from swerving out of control, as Teri shouted, "Yeee-Haaaa…ride-em cowboy!"

I drove straight up Carson Street and turned left onto Los Coyotes Diagonal, as Teri explained which pageantry girls were dating which drummers. "Dave and Lynn have been going out for about a year now," she informed, "and so have Charlie and Evie, but Greg and Patty just got together as well as Mark and Sue…turn right on the first street past Spring." I took Los Coyotes all the way past Spring Street and hung a right into Teri's neighborhood. "Turn left here on Foreman," she said, pointing towards the street sign, "it's 2960 on the left, just a few houses down. So where do you live?"

I told her about my parent's house on Ann Arbor Road and how I had been driving Jeff all across town in the 'McGoo mobile' for the past three weeks so that he could teach me cadences. "Wow, sounds like quite a system," she said with a chuckle, "seems like it worked." I scanned the white painted numbers along the curb until I spotted her address, and then pulled the car up to her house.

"Thanks so much for the ride, Bri," she said, "it was really nice talking to you." Teri then reached over and kissed me on the cheek. She quickly pulled away and said, "Congrats again on making it in the drum section...see you at practice on Tuesday." Before I could react she opened the car door and hopped out, then slammed the door shut and waved. As she crossed the street I quickly rolled down my window and shouted, "Thanks...yes, see you at next practice." She ran up the two steps of her porch, opened the front door and disappeared.

I sat frozen in place for a few seconds, my foot on the brake pedal and the motor idling, my cheek still tingling from Teri's unexpected kiss. *This has to be the best damn day of my life*, I thought, *the best month...the best year!*

Floating on cloud nine, I turned the car around and headed back the way I came towards Lakewood. My body was totally wiped out, my hands a blistered mess, yet I felt completely satisfied. So much had happened in the past few weeks…from the day at Vet's stadium when I first saw the drummers until right this very moment, it seemed that my life had taken a huge turn for the better. *I'm a drummer now*, I thought, *my misfit days are finally over.* My devotion to the drum section and to LBJCB was complete. I couldn't wait to get my band uniform and my very own Ludwig red sparkle tenor drum. I couldn't wait to march my first performance, the Shrine Show, and play cadences as a real drummer!

Who will I ask to sit on the drummer bus with me to the Shrine show, Laura or Teri? I pondered, even though it felt strange to even have such a dilemma. Though I still felt unworthy, I made up my mind who I would ask, knowing that my drummer sweatshirt would help me to find the courage.

I jammed up Spring Street in the night heading west towards Lakewood. I rolled down the window letting the wind blow my hair every which way, feeling totally alive and free. Thinking of Laura, I remembered the red bandana and grabbed it from my back pocket. Raising it out the window high in the air with my fist, I yelled at the top of my lungs to anyone listening, "HAIL TO LBJCB… I AM A DRUMMER!!"

Rob & Brian LBJCB Drummers
(Sweatshirts on Backwards) 1976

EPILOGUE

Standing in front of the full-length mirror in Mrs. Lynd's garage, I admired the reflection of a toy soldier...a teen soldier, dressed in the patriotic colors that were the trademark of a marching band and that made me the newest uniformed member of The Long Beach Junior Concert Band. *Look at you,* I thought excitedly as I struggled with the last button of the stiff new uniform coat, *you're really an LBJCB drummer now!* The grin on the face in the mirror revealed an inner excitement that was barely contained. I reached under the coat and pulled up the sagging band pants, realizing that a belt or suspenders would be needed. With the pants now somewhat straightened, I stared into the mirror again, taking in the dazzling array of colors of the LBJCB uniform...the bright red coat with blue and gold chest-piping, rows of brass buttons on either side, and gold arm braids arching over the LBJCB insignia patches sewn onto each shoulder. There was fancy gold stitching that swirled around each sleeve and the royal blue pants had red and gold stripes running down the sides. The uniform was regal, commanding, and yet festive. *Kind of like a circus ring masters costume,* I thought amusingly, and admired the clean line of the British-style collar across my neck. I beamed back at the toy soldier, his long blond hair now cropped short and the peach-fuzz on his face freshly shaven. *Well McBride,* I thought as I stepped back from the mirror, swinging my arms up as if to play a drum cadence, *time to prove that you can handle the battle of the parade route.* The sleeves of the uniform were tight against my raised arms and it made my stomach tighten…the reality of my first uniformed performance approaching was just starting to sink in.

"Here you go Brian," Mrs. Lynd said, appearing from behind racks of band uniforms that hung in plastic bags in her two-car garage. She handed me the familiar blue and red shako hat with white chin strap and gold eagle emblem glimmering in front. "This is a size seven; that ought to fit your blond head just about right." I took the shako and raised it to my head. "Wait!" Mrs. Lynd shouted, startling me, "we must not forget the finishing touch." She opened a large wooden box that had rows of slots inside, and from one of the slots she pulled out a twelve inch gold feather plume. Holding it by the stick-end she gave it a good shake to fluff it out, and then pushed it into the slot at the top of the shako. "There, try it on now." I positioned the shako onto my head, pulling it snuggly down until the chin strap slid just under my jaw. "Looks perfect," Mrs. Lynd said, "now I'll pin your pants so that we can hem 'em up." She knelt down behind me and began tucking the sagging pant legs in, then pinned them into place at just the right length above the heels.

It was a rainy Saturday afternoon on the first week of March and my Mom had loaned me the Olds wagon for the afternoon so that I could get my uniform and band shoes. With the Shrine show coming up in just one week, there wasn't much time to pull it all together. "There," she said and then stood up, "we'll sew those up and you'll be all set." She motioned towards the makeshift dressing room in the corner, my cue to change out of the uniform. "Now remember, you'll need to get your white band shoes at Knight's Uniform Supply store on Tenth and Atlantic...and you'll also need a pair of red socks."

I glanced one more time at the face in the mirror, noticing how the shako visor made me look tough, like one of those guards at Scotland Yard. *Almost ready to join the ranks of the syncopated drummers.* I thought, my heart filled with pride. Mrs. Lynd then handed me a lime green sheet of paper. "This one is the band roster," she explained, and then handed me a bright pink sheet, "and this one is the band performance schedule." She glanced down the list of band performances for the year. "This sure is a busy year for the band...busiest I've seen. We've got Shrine next week of course, and then there's Las Vegas and Salinas," she flipped over the sheet and continued, "all of the summer and Christmas parades...opening ceremonies for a new ride at

Disneyland called 'Space Mountain'...and not to mention the ham dinner fund-raisers and the annual formal band banquet!"

Mrs. Lynd couldn't have been more correct... 1976 was going to be one crazy year for the Long Beach Junior Concert Band. It was a patriotic year, "The bi-centennial year," as Marvin Marker explained to us, and marching bands like LBJCB were in great demand all over the country. On top of that, Sainburg was having a drummer party the week after the Shrine show and he told me there would be plenty of beer and a 'roundtable session' in his garage, whatever that was... I was also invited to join the guys later at something called 'midnight ramblers,' a secret meeting place in the back of the Arby's parking lot where the LBJCB trucks were parked. This was the spot where the drummers parked their muscle cars and hung out, "eating Jack-in-the-Box and shooting the bull all night," as Rob had described it.

As their newest rookie tenor drummer, I couldn't wait to jump in with both feet. The uniform and drum were my battle gear, but the brown and gold sweatshirt would be my all-season pass to the fun...my entry into the intense, comical and outrageous world of the drummers. With the gusto of a pirate setting sail for the Caribbean Isles, I was open to anything and everything. At long last I felt that I *belonged*...and for this, the drummers had my undying loyalty.

Yes 1976 was a year that I would never forget. What followed in the weeks and months ahead were beyond my wildest imagination. But that my friends, is a story for another day...